Producer
eBookPro Publishing
www.ebook-pro.com

TIMEFULNESS
Amir Peled

Written in Israel, Denmark
Copyright © 2023 by Amir Peled

Chief Editor: Tony Maxwell

Translated and edited by: Jonathan Boxman and Amir Peled

Final English editing: Anna Leah Berstein Simpson,
Dr. Ori Weisberg, Amir Peled

Artwork: Amir Peled, Luana Lourenço

Contact: becometimeful@gmail.com

ISBN 9798868447044

TIMEFULNESS

Why Successful People
Don't Match Their Socks

A Simple, Proven Guide to Success

AMIR PELED

Contents

PART I

UNLOCK TIMEFULNESS

Your Ultimate Key to Success

1. **Meet Emily**
   A First Step to Thinking Like Einstein 9

2. **Decoding Success**
   Lessons from Eighteen Years in Israel's Startup
   Scene and Beyond 13

3. **Time Coins**
   The Hidden Currency Shaping Your Life 17

4. **How to Become Serially Successful**
   A Five-Step Plan 26

PART II

MASTER TIMEFULNESS

Seven Strategies to Transform Your Life and Career

5. **Focus Like Jobs**
   STRATEGY I 42

6. **Produce Like Picasso**
   STRATEGY II 49

7. **Capitalize Like Franklin**
   STRATEGY III 55

8. **Lead Like Schwab**
   STRATEGY IV 63

9. **Envision Like Musk**
    STRATEGY V   70

10. **Futurecast Like Buffett**
    STRATEGY VI   79

11. **Select Like Cornett**
    STRATEGY VII   90

PART III
BEYOND STRATEGIES
Become Serially Successful

12. **Master Your Inner Compass**
    A Guide to Timeful Decision-Making   111

13. **Designing Your Life**
    A Step-by-Step Guide   117

14. **Love Like Lincoln**
    Romance and The Shortcut to Success   122

15. **The End Game**
    Your Timeful Path to Serial Success   129

Afterword   137

Challenge Yourself and Others   138

Glossary   140

Acknowledgements   144

PART I

UNLOCK TIMEFULNESS: YOUR ULTIMATE KEY TO SUCCESS

MEET EMILY
A FIRST STEP TO
THINKING LIKE EINSTEIN

Let's talk about socks for a moment. Socks as literal socks, but also as a metaphor.

Meet John,[1] a thirty-year-old who pairs his socks, each with its intended mate. We don't judge John for this. It's neither good nor bad. Pairing your socks has advantages and disadvantages.

Albert Einstein, on the other hand, is Albert Einstein. Probably the only non-clown of his time who didn't pair his socks. When asked about this strange habit, he replied: "Life is too short to waste time pairing socks."[2] He had his own view of how time should be spent.

Now take *Emily*.[3] Emily is no Einstein, but she isn't John either. Emily is something else. She realizes that she spends ten extra minutes every week searching through her socks to pair them. When she does, something troubles her. Something tells her it doesn't make sense, that there must be a better, smarter way. She's heard of Einstein's sock quote, but she doesn't want to be considered an anomaly.

Emily estimates that she spends 520 minutes a year pairing her socks. Not ten minutes pass before she orders fourteen

---

1. The name John was randomly picked.

2. Len Fisher, "Why Einstein didn't wear socks and the nature of scientific inquiry," ABC Radio National, May 11, 2016.

3. The name Emily was randomly picked.

pairs of black socks for work, another fourteen pairs of white socks for running, and fourteen pairs of red fluffy socks for use on cold nights.

As a result of this, Emily switches from doing laundry once a week to once every two weeks. She stuffs all the socks together into her drawer and simply grabs two of the same color as she needs them. But she doesn't only save forty minutes a month by making this change. The shift in perspective opens up a whole new world of opportunities for her.

She toys with the idea that she could maybe close the gap between her and Einstein in more ways than just this sock business. She begins to wonder if there are other areas of her life where she could identify unproductive patterns and change them to her advantage.

In the following, we will argue that this sock-pairing case divides human behavior into three typical patterns. The John pattern, where we do something today simply because we did it yesterday, because of what we've studied, or because of social norms. We aren't normally inclined to stop and ponder better, more productive options. We often do whatever springs to mind—we follow our "most accessible thought."[4]

Then there's the Einstein pattern, where we tend to do the smartest thing every time, a pattern we will refer to here as serially successful.

Finally, there is Emily's pattern. Emily is searching for a better way. And she understands that a better way just might have

---

4. We will be using the phrase "accessible thought" to designate thoughts that are the most accessible to us. These are thoughts that tend to pop up in our mind and serve us quickly (for good or bad). Daniel Kahneman, who uses the term "availability heuristics" when discussing accessible thought, notes that the fact that such thoughts are easily accessible compels us to adopt them, but that this does not necessarily mean they are the best or most effective thoughts. Daniel Kahneman, Thinking, Fast and Slow (New York: Farrar, Straus and Giroux, 2011).

something to do with the way she spends her time. She's not too concerned about what others think of her choices or other distractions from her determination to do the right things, to succeed, to improve and to make the lives of her dear ones and her own as good as they can be. Emily means business. And in that sense, she is probably like many readers of this book. Emily sometimes gets it wrong. But she often gets it right. She often has at least something in common with Einstein. And you probably have it too. In fact, Emily's path to success started with figuring out what it is exactly that we all share with Einstein.

To start this journey, Emily asked one simple question. The million-dollar question: "Are there cases where we are all Einsteins? Cases in which we all pick the best option?"

THE EINSTEIN EFFECT

The world's population has reached eight billion. Some of us do radical, even crazy things. But there are some things no one does or will ever do. No one has ever woken up in the morning looking for a traffic jam to get stuck in. No one has ever overloaded a suitcase on purpose just to be charged extra by an airline. We will all choose the shortest route suggested by our navigation app when heading to the office.

When the rewards and penalties are crystal clear, we are all unanimous in our choices. In fact, a central argument of this book is that when we see clearly that we will either win or lose time, or improve or degrade the quality of our time, we are all the same—smart, efficient and in agreement. We are all Einsteins.

<u>CHAPTER RECAP</u>

- When facing a case like the need to match socks, we lean towards the easy, obvious choice—our accessible thought, but the choice to match our socks, like any other choice we make, is in fact an opportunity to gain or waste time, or quality of time and even an opportunity to change our perspective.
- When it comes to life's clear opportunities to gain or lose time (or time quality), we all know how to act.

DECODING SUCCESS
LESSONS FROM EIGHTEEN YEARS IN ISRAEL'S STARTUP SCENE AND BEYOND

This book is not an academic work. I'm writing simply as a human being who, initially, never even intended to address a wider audience. I wrote mainly for myself, my family, and a few sympathetic friends.

But the book hasn't come from nowhere, either. I worked for eighteen years in Israel's renowned startup scene, mainly in the tech and medical fields across thirteen industries for companies ranging from a small AI startup to a Nasdaq-traded leader in medical devices.

I was fortunate enough to be able to work closely with many uniquely talented people who achieved great success. And during this time, I found myself thinking a lot about these people, noticing what they had in common, and learning everything I could from them.

Eight years into my career, I felt I was onto something. That I had cracked if not the code—well at least a code to how these people I admired operated, what was really driving them. I started to see parallels between some of these figures and a great number of successful people from different countries and historical periods—people that all of us are familiar with.

This led to a ten-year journey of exploring similarities and looking for patterns behind these people's behavior. Along the way, I was surprised to discover that they all shared certain attitudes and behaviors that helped explained their success. Even more exciting, they seemed to share these attitudes and behaviors with practically all of the world's most famous success stories. The more I learned, the more I saw a single principle start to emerge.

THE BOOK'S STRUCTURE

Timefulness is divided into three parts. Part I presents my thesis that there is a single governing principle behind all human success.

Part II takes a closer look at what we will call "serially successful people," the people who succeed repeatedly, even in different fields. It defines the strategies they employ to design great products or lead great companies and communities, and helps flesh out the single unifying principle behind their success and ours.

The last part of the book demonstrates how we can implement this principle in our everyday life: When trying to choose the right path, making important decisions and seeking personal and professional growth.

AUTHOR'S NOTE

The order of the chapters in this book and the examples of success we present can be further discussed, criticized and perhaps adjusted. Where I have chosen Benjamin Franklin, I could have chosen David Goggins instead. Both exemplify a key point in this book—if you succeed in one field, you can repeat it in many others too by being aware of the common root of all human success. Similarly, Marie Curie could easily replace Steve Jobs and Bill Gates, perhaps Elon Musk too. Each of us has our own perspective on the world, on different people and on what success (and life) is all about.

Although I immersed myself in ten years of research and five full years of writing, I still don't know everything about the figures you'll read about, their successes and failures. And of course, there will be other success stories that you know and find more appropriate than those chosen for the journey we are about to take together along this book.

But there is one thing I do know. The stories in this book offer more than enough knowledge and insights to enable you embark on your own journey towards success. More importantly, this book is not about how to succeed in one field or another, it's about how to become the embodiment of success—how to become what we'll be calling serially successful.

Your favorite or most useful chapter could very well depend on where you're at in life, the point in your life where you encounter this book, and the ease with which you'll be able to identify with the figures presented here.

The similarities you'll find can change at any given point and hopefully you'll see the people mentioned in this book and their successes as well as yours in different light every time you read this book—which I hope would be more than once, as I believe a book not worth reading more than once isn't worth reading at all.5

As you read, try to remember, it's not about those people and their successes—it's about you and what you'll make of it. It's about who you will become once you complete the reading of this book and use it as your own for the successes you choose to pursue and for the person you wish to be.

---

5. Karl Julius Weber, David Shaham (editor), The Book of Quotations (Keter: Jerusalem)—Hebrew print only.

TIME COINS
THE HIDDEN CURRENCY
SHAPING YOUR LIFE

In this book, we'll call what Einstein has, what Emily works towards, and what John sometimes struggles to earn, keep or enhance Time Coins. Time coins are a portion of our life. They represent chunks of time, with the value we assign that time. Why do we need a concept like time coins? Because the formula that leads us in life (and success in life), a formula we'll introduce in the next chapter, shows that although we think we're striving for a romantic partner, a career, good health, or happiness, we're actually seeking the same thing: A valuable time coin. It's a significant product of a given period of time multiplied by the value we attribute to that time, which we refer to as a time coin—the coin of life.

There might be other ways of dividing time into segments or viewing life, but it's this way that may help us focus in life's basic building blocks—time and its value while remembering that time is essentially also a currency, allowing us to gain, save, protect, stipulate and trade it to better our life—invest it wisely and make more and better time, diminish its value or lose it.

Now let's take a look at the two main types of time coins.

POSITIVE AND NEGATIVE TIME COINS

Positive time coins are the result of clearly beneficial choices, thoughts, feelings or actions. These create (or can create) a clearly positive impact on our lives, such as when we enjoy a good laugh or find money on the sidewalk.

Negative time coins are the result of choices, thoughts, feelings or actions that clearly waste our time, diminish its quality or even make our life shorter. We don't need Einstein's intelligence or Emily's analysis to know that these are choices to be avoided. We are all geniuses when it comes to clearly positive and negative time coins.

But what about cases that aren't so clear cut? These are cases where we set up businesses and other ventures whose benefits are hard to predict. When we involve ourselves in activities with less obvious costs and benefits, we sometimes win and sometimes lose. When we invest in stocks, gamble in a casino, vote for a political party, choose a romantic partner or select a place of work, it's hard to tell for sure whether we'll gain or lose. And we struggle to make the right choices.

So why is this? When is the road to success so clear that we are unanimous in choosing it, and the road to failure so obvious that most of us would not take it in our right minds? And when do we face more complex crossroads that divide us into Johns, Emilys, and Einsteins?

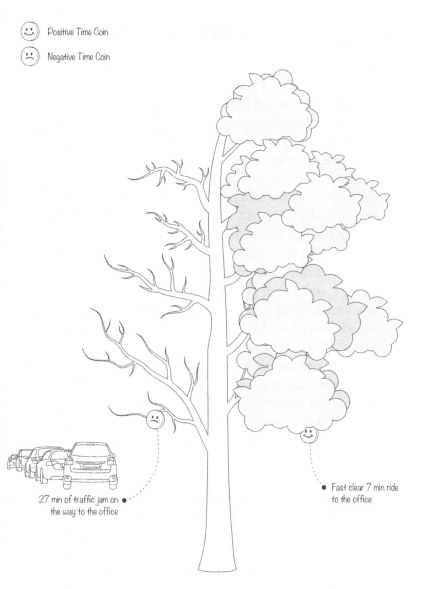

Positive Time Coin

Negative Time Coin

27 min of traffic jam on the way to the office

Fast clear 7 min ride to the office

Figure 1: Positive and Negative Time Coins
Choosing a fast route to the office is an example of a clearly positive time coin, while getting into traffic is a clearly negative time coin.

CHALLENGING TIME COINS

As we established, when the rewards and penalties are crystal clear, we are all unanimous in our choices. When our navigation app offers us two routes, one that will take seven minutes, or one that will take twenty-seven minutes, the choice is easy. And when some product we consume regularly is on sale at half price, we know how to act.

The problems start when it's harder to calculate the costs and benefits of the different paths we could choose to follow. For example, if we had known that the new phone we just bought because it was fifty dollars cheaper would force us to spend a day taking it to be fixed, another two hours replacing a broken screen, and minutes wasted on slow charging every day, we would have gladly paid a little extra (in either money or research time) for a better model. But it's hard to make a sound choice based on nothing but a flashy ad, an attractive device, a list of features and a lower price.

In this situation, we are faced with a challenge more complex than picking a shorter route over a longer one, simply because the link between our choice to its impact on our time is not obvious. As we rush to another meeting, to a date, or to pick up the kids, we don't have the time, patience or ability to think like Einstein (or Emily).

If you think about it, the choices we make about socks, telephones and so on are really choices about our time. And as this book will argue, our time is our life—and the choices we make about time are quite literally choices that define our lives.

Life, beyond its mere biological meaning, is simply the time we have, and the meaning we ascribe to that time. It's a huge number of different segments of time that can be more or less positive. From breathtaking seconds or "a good time," to a decent year or a very successful decade. These segments of time (positive and negative, challenging or straightforward) are the time coins that make up our life.

Given that this is the case, it only follows that, to succeed in life, we need to focus on time. We need to protect it, gain more of it, or color as much of it in as positive hues as we can. In other words, the game of life is a game in which we need to acquire as many positive time coins as we can and avoid the negative ones.

But life isn't always a walk in the park. When our complex verbal thinking, strong visual impressions or just plain complexity hide the true value of an opportunity—the amount and quality of time coins it helps us win—we doubt. When we struggle to see the clear costs and benefits of our possible choices, then we stumble.

Facing some challenging time coins, we might worry we'll need to invest too much to acquire them. And if we don't enjoy an investment of time, the time can feel like an eternity. Plus, for long-term investments, there is so much that can go sideways that success is rarely guaranteed from the outset. And it's hard to feel good about investing when the rewards feel uncertain. Some of these challenging cases are likely to turn out well, but cause us discomfort or even pain. They require us to invest considerable time while experiencing mixed emotions and worrying that our investment might not pay off—these are what we can call positive challenging time coins.

Then there's another type of challenging time coin, far less likely to provide genuine value. Usually the opposite. These can include driving recklessly, smoking or cheating. They are temptations we struggle to resist because they offer a high probability immediate gain with a long-term risk that might never materialize, but they rarely pay off in the long term. These are negative challenging time coins.

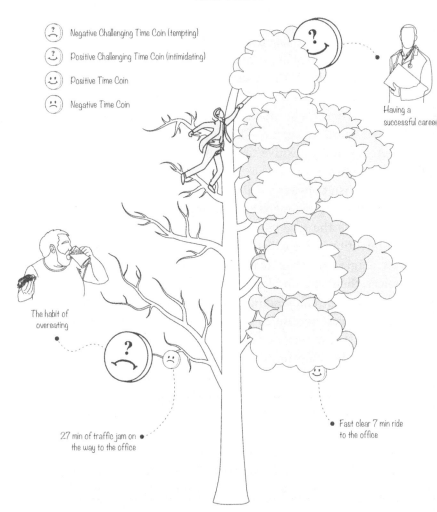

Negative Challenging Time Coin (tempting)

Positive Challenging Time Coin (intimidating)

Positive Time Coin

Negative Time Coin

Having a
successful career

The habit of
overeating

27 min of traffic jam on
the way to the office

Fast clear 7 min ride
to the office

Figure 2: Clear and Challenging Time Coins
In addition to the two clearly positive and negative time coins presented
in figure 1, figure 2 shows an example of a challenging negative time coin
(overeating), which is a "low-hanging" habit. It's a challenging negative
time coin because it is both a low-hanging fruit and counterintuitive—it
feels easy and good for the short term but tends to have a negative impact
on our life overall. On the other hand, a challenging positive time coin
(in this case, having a successful career) tends to be a high-hanging fruit.
It requires a massive, long-term, not-always pleasant and sometimes-
intimidating effort and yields no certainty of success.

TIME-COIN WEALTH

Clearly positive, clearly negative, and challenging for good or bad, these time coins comprise our entire experienced life. In this book, we will refer to the sum total of our existing time coins at any given moment as our time-coin wealth.

And yet there is more to the story than the time-coin wealth we have already accumulated. There is also wealth we can gain (or lose) in the future, by investing time today in what we hope will be time coin wins down the road.

In other words, the "secret" to success is to effectively leverage our time-coin wealth—trade the time we have to gain more or better time. So, how do we do it? And how can we do it even better?

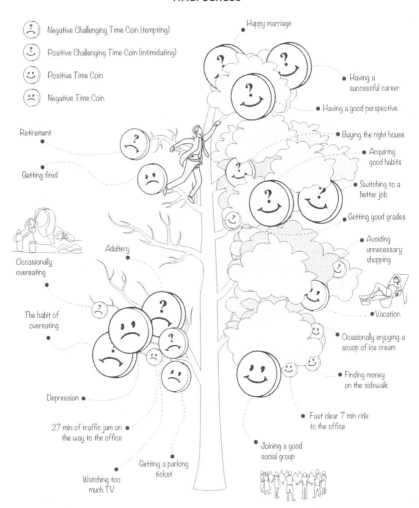

Figure 3: Our Time Coin Wealth

The left side of the tree holds a few of life's typical negative time coins while the right side presents the typically positive ones. The problem is that some of life's most positive time coins (usually those with the highest impact), tend to be challenging, intimidating high-hanging fruits requiring significant effort and investment. On the other hand, the challenging negative time coins, those we are sometimes tempted to see as positive or to pursue without too much thinking, tend to be low-hanging fruits with a high probability of imme-diate positive impact (and usually long-term negative impact).

CHAPTER RECAP

1. All of life's opportunities can be divided into the following categories:

   - Positive time coins—easy, obvious opportunities we all tend to spot and seize.
   - Negative time coins—easy, obvious opportunities we all tend to avoid.
   - Positive challenging time coins—valuable prizes that tend to require an unknown, challenging or uncomfortable investment—life's high hanging fruits.
   - Negative challenging time coins—immediately satisfying opportunities that tend to have longer-term negative effects or an overall negative impact—often low hanging fruits.

2. The sum total of all the time coins we have at a given moment is our time-coin wealth.

3. The way to succeed in life is to trade or leverage our time-coin wealth and increase its value.

HOW TO BECOME
SERIALLY SUCCESSFUL
A FIVE-STEP PLAN

An ancient tale demonstrates how hard it could be to use our time wisely when it comes to life's challenging cases—when our instincts, shaped by years of evolution, sometimes lead us astray, especially in a modern world filled with choices unknown to our ancestors. A common version of the tale goes as follows:

> Moses, raised as a young child in the Egyptian palace, once made a move that hinted at a destiny far grander than anyone might have predicted— he took Pharaoh's crown and placed it on his own head. This act stirred whispers among advisors, with some suggesting he aspired to the throne. Jethro, however, proposed a test to discern Moses's intentions. Presented with gold—a selection symbolizing hunger for power—and coal—standing for innocence—Moses, instinctively reached for the gold, avoiding the burning coal. Yet, in a divine twist, the angel Gabriel moved his hand to the coal, saving his life but marking him with a speech impediment, as Moses swiftly placed his burnt finger in his mouth.[6]

---

6. Exodus Rabbah 1:31.

Whether Moses knew it or not, what he faced was a challenging time coin which could have cost him his life. Navigating life's challenges (consciously or not) often feels like choosing between the gold and the coal. Even when it comes to mundane decisions like changing jobs, the feeling could be similar. With the presence of the unknown, we are challenged with making a wise choice in unfavorable circumstances and often have to rely on instinct. But what if we could hone our instincts? Perhaps even to a level that would enable us to choose and deal with challenging time coins as skillfully as we handle the clearly positive and negative ones? To facilitate that lucrative goal of becoming master time traders, even when dealing with life's challenging cases, consider success as a mathematical formula:

Success = time coin wealth profit = better life =
(time coin gains – time coin investment) x probability –
of winning – time coin losses x risk

Complex? Yes. But what happens when things get complex? Our brain seeks simplicity. We try to simplify this success formula, or governing principle, as we will call it, along with the complexity of the situation. Instead of considering gains, investment, chances, losses and risks, we focus on just one thing—whatever our brain perceives as the greatest, most obvious opportunity to gain or lose time coins (the biggest time coin in mind). Or, any arbitrary distraction that could put an end to our feeling of inconvenience. It's a time and energy-saving defense mechanism that "helps us" not to get stuck, delay, or think too hard when we might not have to. But it's also where we leave piles of time (and money) on the table. It's our critical juncture, our "gold or coal" moment.

How do we navigate it?

Very few people like formulas. And the success formula presented here won't be our main go-to solution. The key point is to be aware of the way our governing principle drives us from within by the force of instinct, an instinct we can hone. After all, the tale about Moses isn't about an adult Moses but about young Moses—a child. As grownups, we can better control and enhance our instincts. To start doing that, even just one example and a couple of tries at using the formula could suffice.

Consider the following case: Elon Musk spent $90,000 to ship by a private jet a component needed for a rocket just to save a day in the timeline. Make sense? Hardly. But Musk reasoned that the expenditure was nothing, given that he projected it would allow SpaceX to start earning ten million dollars a day, one day sooner, ten years down the road.[7] Now, how would the numbers add up in our success formula?

Investment = $90,000
Losses = $90,000
Gains = 10,000,000
Probability of winning = 0.99
Risk = 0.01

$9,910,000 = ($10,000,000-$90,000) x 0.99 – $90,000x0.01

The total time-coin profit and level of success—in this case presented as money—would be $9,910,000 (plus the fame, inspiration for his team, influence and more...).

The magic number here, which we can also call the serially successful factor, is 0.99. If Musk hadn't felt absolutely certain

---

7. Ashlee Vance, *Elon Musk: Tesla, SpaceX, and the Quest for a Fantastic Future* (Harper Audio, May 19, 2015).

that SpaceX would succeed at so great a scale that $90,000 would be a minor investment, he wouldn't have been able to make it. He needed to be either absolutely sure that it was going to work, or perfectly fine with the financial, mental and social loss.

Now, imagine what we could do with this mode of thinking. What could we discover if we chose to ask ourselves a similar question: How can I achieve the same scale of win turning $90,000 into $10,000,000, even if I don't have that much money?

Should you choose to employ such a deliberate thought process, what would you find out? You would probably quickly notice that it forces you to identify significant gains before devoting yourself to an initiative. It encourages you to find the power to step out of your daily routine and ask: How can I invest just one hour and gain a time coin that would easily be worth hundreds or thousands of hours? Maybe calling your elderly parents and listening to their favorite childhood stories will one day become your most precious hour. Perhaps renewing contact with an old friend would be, or working on your CV, choosing a financial investment or starting to work out.

If you lay such opportunities down with their five parameters specifying how much time and time quality you could gain, lose, risk and need to invest, and what your chances of creating a precious moment, acquiring a new habit or shifting the course of your life would be, you would increase the chances to choose and do right. You can more easily question some of the less valuable things you might occupy yourself with, and stick to something valuable—even when it seems counterintuitive.

HOW TO STREAMLINE
AND DUPLICATE YOUR SUCCESSES
ONE STEP AT A TIME

Behavioral economics researchers Daniel Kahneman and Amos Tversky found dozens of cognitive biases.[8] Each could easily lead us away from success at any given moment. Luckily, with experience, we get better at making many, but not all, decisions. As Economics Nobel Laureate Richard Thaler explains, we mainly get better at the decisions we take frequently.[9] These decisions are typically the small, mundane, less impactful ones: Which coffee to drink or how many boxes of milk to buy for the week. With the other, often more impactful type of decisions (whom to marry, how many kids to have, what to study, where to live and work), we can't rely on extensive experience and well-based knowledge, simply because we don't make these decisions very often. We don't have the needed experience or knowledge to sense, let alone estimate, our profit, risk and losses. These opportunities are challenging time coins that typically hide the full implications of dealing with them while requiring a significant long-term effort.

This is where the success formula becomes a game changer. If the most precious thing in life is your time, its meaning and quality, or that of your dear ones, and if everything you do or choose in life has an impact on your time, what would happen, if you began considering a growing number of decisions from one main perspective focused on, well, TIME?

Thaler's important explanation of why you are highly successful, and in fact serially successful, when it comes to

---

8. Daniel Kahneman and co-authors, Rationality fairness, happiness—selected articles (Keter: Jerusalem, 2005)—only printed in Hebrew.

9. Richard H. Thaler, Cass R. Sunstein, *Nudge* (Yale: New Haven, 2009).

picking up your favorite milk, but possibly less serially successful in other fields, would no longer apply to you. You would have started your journey from being what Thaler calls a "good decision architect,"[10] specializing in milk, wine, or perhaps Nasdaq stocks, relationships or leadership, to becoming a good decision architect of everything.

With every decision you take—big or small, you will hone your ability to categorize, quantify or assess opportunities. You'll be boosting your intuition and instincts with regards to the one truly important coin of life—your time and its quality. And here is how to do it step by step.

FIVE STEPS TO BECOMING SERIALLY SUCCESSFUL

STEP 1 — PREDICT

You predict your time coin gains. How do you do it? In any effective way you find reliable. Sometimes it's your instincts, other times you'll need a more analytical approach, such as categorizing an opportunity as a positive or negative time coin, or quantifying it to estimate your profit using the success formula. By doing so, you gain clarity. You take a time coin, and bring it closer to being a clearly positive or negative time coin—the point where we are all Einsteins. That's not to say it's all easy and fun from that point on. It's still a challenging time coin, but now that you have a clearer picture of your expected gains, you are far more likely to make sound choices, stick to your effort and succeed.

---

10. Thaler, *Nudge*.

STEP 2 — SELECT OR INVENT

Once you have your assessment or vision (which we have called prediction), you can more easily compare it to other options, select it, or make the effort to invent an alternative.

STEP 3 — INVEST

After you've made your selection, you obviously need to get the job done. That means investing time and time-equivalent resources such as effort, money, collaboration and dedication. You need to focus on your selected time coin and effectively invest enough time in it.

STEP 4 — COLLECT AND REFLECT

Following your effective investment in a valuable time coin, you'll usually reap the winnings. That's the time to collect and enjoy the fruits of your effort, and also to reflect, which will allow you to take your new experience and use it to better predict, select (or invent), and invest in future opportunities.

STEP 5 — REPEAT

After collecting and reflecting, you can repeat the process, leveraging your success to make it better or more effective, or discover how to apply it to seemingly different opportunities and make them successful too.

HOW TO CREATE THE EINSTEIN EFFECT

Once you've gone through this process: Predict—select (or invent)—invest—collect (and reflect)—repeat, while focusing on the common grounds of different opportunities (time and its quality), you are not just gaining valuable experience, but you win something else too. You are calibrating your governing principle towards a different magnitude of effectiveness. Getting closer to a point where you can instinctively spot and seize life's more valuable prizes and do so consistently. You become able to take more adequate choices and follow through, even when not consciously analyzing opportunities, working with formulas or thinking of time coins—you made your choice simpler and easier.

The serially successful people you'll encounter in the following chapters, do many different things in different ways, but ultimately it all boils down to predicting the value of a time coin, selecting it (or inventing a new source of time coins), effectively working to get it (our investing stage) and then collecting and reflecting. They then repeat the process, stick to their selection for the long run, or find other valuable options—but they haven't just succeeded, they also became more successful. And this is our offering for you: Follow the process a few times to get a few more successes—knowledge, insights, experience, connections, funds, reputation, or moments of joy. Then, leverage those achievements to further compound your time-coin wealth—to build a better life that you couldn't have built without those achievements. In parallel (with time and repetition), your new experience—your ability to assess opportunities and orchestrate your investments—will become second nature. You'll be able to consistently win as much as you can using your analytical skills, but also without giving it too much thought. You'll be getting it right almost every time, even when it's extremely challenging. This is how you become serially successful.

It's at this stage where you gain an ability to look through life's complex matrix and see opportunities for what they are—a source of more or less time-coin wealth. Like Einstein, you could now look at socks (as well as more valuable things) and see time—your time, the way it flows and the way you want it to flow.

BUILDING A LEGACY OF SUCCESS

If we visualize our choices, we see that they aren't mere points on a line but steps on a ladder. And the goal is to keep climbing. As Newton said, "If I have seen further, it is by standing on the shoulders of giants." Where Newton meant standing on the shoulders of someone who achieved success in the past, we would argue that the best shoulders to stand on are those of your former self. Your current self will then become another giant—upon whose shoulders your future self will rise. Be that giant. Improve with every step you take. Life is more than habits or luck. It's about seizing moments that add value to our life. But it's also about boosting your experience, knowledge, instincts and resources. Accumulating the tools that will take you to the tipping point where you become serially successful—continuously making better predictions and investments, creating successes when you are being analytic and systematic, but also when you aren't. As you cycle through this process you don't only build a legacy of success—you become a success.

###

Share with the world your "gold or coal" moments and the cases where past investment allowed you to stand taller and reach higher. Use #timefulness #goldorcoal #bethatgiant #becomeasuccess.

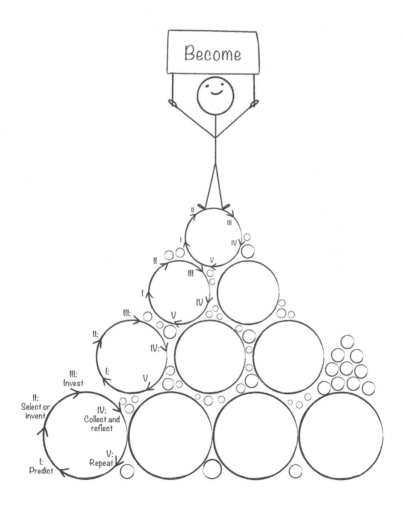

Figure 4: How to Increase Your Time-Coin Wealth and Become Serially Successful
Follow the five steps to amass valuable time coins (large and small) into your time-coin wealth: (I) Predict, (II) Select or invent, (III) Invest, (IV) Collect and reflect, (V) Repeat. Continue the process until you become serially successful in the field/s of your choice.

CHAPTER RECAP

- Success means generating time-coin profit.

- Becoming more successful means being able to consistently generate time coin gains while avoiding losses.

- The Five Steps to become serially successful are:
  1. **Predict:** Anticipate valuable time coin gains.
  2. **Select or Invent:** Choose or envision the right time coins.
  3. **Invest:** Work effectively to get your time coins.
  4. **Collect and Reflect:** Secure your time coin and reflect on your success to level up your analytical thinking and instincts.
  5. **Repeat:** Leverage your past successes to double in on new or existing opportunities.

- Once you execute these five steps enough times, while focusing on their common denominator—time and its value, you gain a critical mass of experience which you'll naturally shift into a gut feeling, intuition and instincts making you more consistently successful—seizing opportunities not only when you're concentrating, at your best, experienced, or lucky, but many other times too. You can become successful even when you're in a hurry, tired, hungry or dealing with a "completely" new challenge, simply because for you, there will be no brand-new challenge.

PART I RECAP

PART I Unlock Timefulness: Your Ultimate Key to Success.	
1. Meet Emily	Every opportunity either allows us to gain or lose time, as well as affecting the quality of that time. When it comes to life's clear opportunities to gain or lose time (or time quality), we all know how to act.
2. Decoding Success	My personal story.
3. Time Coins	The sum total of all the time coins we have at a given moment is our time-coin wealth. The way to succeed in life is to trade or leverage our time-coin wealth and increase its value.
4. How to Become Serially Successful A Five-Step Plan	When facing a challenging opportunity, assess its value by categorizing it as one of the four types of time coins. Alternatively, you can quantify its profit or use your intuition. Then, follow the five steps: Predict, select (or invent), invest, collect (and reflect) and repeat—if you seize your opportunity, that's great, if not, you've achieved something no less valuable. With proper reflection and repetition, you'll approach the next opportunity with higher abilities, better instincts and all in all greater success chances. Follow the process.
PART II Master Timefulness: Seven Strategies to Transform Your Life and Career.	
PART III Beyond Strategies: Become Serially Successful.	

MAKE IT YOUR OWN

Most people need to experience some sort of dramatic event to change their life—an accident, hearing God, a tough breakup or an epiphany. Our feelings and thoughts need to collide with such force that they can literally blow us off the path we're on and land us on another.

But there's another way too. Making the effort to better predict the value of life's challenging cases. Not that it would solve everything, mind you. It wouldn't necessarily make the voyage easy or fun, and it wouldn't guarantee that you'd even pursue a great opportunity. But it can increase the chances that you'll go for it, follow through, and succeed.

While there's always a chance that you'll be struck by a profound realization, that epiphany might never arrive. Fortunately, there's a simple way to gain this insight through deliberate effort that really doesn't have to take more than a day of business as usual or even a twenty-minute break. Ready to try it?

Set aside at least twenty minutes. Start by choosing some of the goals you are working towards. Now write down how much time you are likely to invest in achieving each goal and rate the quality of the time you expect to invest. Then estimate the amount of time you expect the achievement to provide for you or for others, and rate the quality of that time. Consider each goal's profit in time coins—the amount of positive time you'll end up adding to your life. Then prioritize those offering the highest profit measured in time coins.

If you like using technological tools, consider using ChatGPT or a similar AI-based tool. Type in these four prompts:

1. What are some things I could do to save or improve the quality of my time?
2. Where could I invest my time or other resources that would be likely to give me or my loved ones a significantly higher return?
3. Quantify the amount of time I'll have to invest in the different options you suggested, and the amount of time or time derivatives, such as the money they can generate or their impact on the quality of my time and life.
4. List the opportunities in order of profit.

As you read the tool's responses, you'll sense that you get a better vibe from some of the suggestions. Take these to the next level by providing information about yourself and asking follow-up questions until you've generated your personal insightful revelation. Then, continue the conversation to figure out how to seize these opportunities most effectively.

CHALLENGE YOURSELF AND OTHERS

Use #timefulness to share your discoveries, letting people know about quantified clear wins and alerting them to losses using #timecrime or #timefulmess. Here are a couple of examples:

1. Improving your negotiation skills is likely to earn you an average extra $5,000 every year.[11]
2. The average person types about 40 words a minute.[12] By learning "blind typing" (free investment of 5–20 hours), you should be able to boost your speed to 70 words a minute, saving up to 1.5 hours every day. In parallel, incorporate AI into your writing (and reading) and save even more while improving the quality of your work.

Once you've discussed the quantified opportunities above with Chat GPT or a similar tool, try asking for more such useful quantifications until you feel like you found a valuable enough opportunity to pursue.

---

11. Michelle Marks and Crystal Harold, *Journal of Organizational Behavior*, Vol. 32, No. 3 (April 2011), pp. 371-394.

12. Karat et al.

PART II

MASTER TIMEFULNESS: SEVEN STRATEGIES TO TRANSFORM YOUR LIFE AND CAREER

FOCUS LIKE JOBS
(STRATEGY I)

*God gave me the stubbornness of a mule
and a fairly keen scent*
Albert Einstein[13]

It's not common human behavior to approach the world focusing almost exclusively on a single goal or activity. When we're afraid or insecure, we gravitate to choices that alleviate our fears. When we're in pain, we tend to embrace any option that will let us opt out of our suffering. And when we're enjoying ourselves, it's not always easy to pause to consider potential long-term consequences.

Nonetheless, the lives of serially successful people suggest a different approach. If we examine them carefully, we can discern decisions and behaviors that are typical and indicative of them, a sign that they possess an extraordinary ability (or will) to focus on one thing—one time coin—where most of us spread our investments more thinly across numerous coins.

In this chapter, we'll refer to that one single time coin as a person's "ace" time coin, and we'll call the strategy of single-mindedly pursuing such a time coin "Focus like Jobs." This

13. Whitrow, G.J. Einstein: The Man and His Achievement. New York: Dover, 1967 (founded through: Alice Calaprice (collected and edited), *The Quotable Einstein*, The Hebrew University of Jerusalem and Princeton University Press, 1996, Hed Arzi Publishing House, Or Yehuda 1999.

strategy has been applied by different people in a variety of fields. Two people who can help us understand this strategy lived in different periods, worked in different fields, and had very different public personae: Albert Einstein and Steve Jobs.

Yet even a glance at Einstein's and Job's physical appearance suggests a shared strategy. Einstein either didn't wear socks or wore socks that didn't match—two odd behaviors that drew much attention. When pressed regarding his sense of fashion, or lack thereof, the brilliant scientist who revealed the secrets of time and space replied that life was too short to waste time matching socks.[14] Steve Jobs went further, often walking barefoot. Einstein didn't waste time on haircuts, and Jobs didn't bother selecting new shirts for Apple's product launches.

One could argue that these habits represent only negligible savings of time, or that such habits concerning dress are superficial and coincidental. These preferences can also be seen as individual trademarks with no bearing on time-saving, focus or perspectives on life. But socks and combs weren't the only things Einstein and Jobs avoided to protect their time and focus it around one main effort.

In addition to shying away from spending time on shirts and shoes, Jobs also cultivated a furniture-less house.[15] This was not only about saving time he would have lost choosing, purchasing, and arranging furniture, or the time equivalent of the furniture's purchase price. A furniture-free home is reminiscent of a discovery by Economics Nobel Laureate Daniel Kahneman, who pointed out the importance of thoughts that tend to pop-up in one's mind (our accessible thoughts).[16] Based on Kahneman's findings, we could

---

14. Fisher, "Why Einstein didn't wear socks."

15. Walter Isaacson, *Steve Jobs* (New York, Simon & Schuster: 2011).

16. Kahneman, *Rationality fairness, happiness—selected articles.*

conclude that if our home has fewer furnishings, our mind might have fewer distractions.

You could still argue that the time savings represented by shirts, socks, haircuts and furniture, and guarding our minds from other distracting thoughts, don't add up to the critical mass of time required to achieve significant success. But to the skilled eye, not investing time in shirts, haircuts, socks or even shoes, all represents the same phenomenon. They're a window into a different perspective. A perspective where success isn't seen as the result of this or that preference, saving a minute here and there, but the result of a single-minded determination to collect or create more time or higher-quality time.

Two other highly successful individuals who have employed the strategy of focusing in a single valuable time coin are Jeff Bezos and Elon Musk.

In the early days of Amazon, Bezos and a handful of his first employees took down the door to his parents' garage just to acquire a table as fast as they could.[17] Bezos and his coworkers sought to improve the painful and inefficient experience of packing books while bent down on the floor. The decision turned out to be very efficient. They didn't have to waste time selecting, purchasing, and transporting a table, as they already had the door. When we are extremely focused on the value of certain time coins, it's easier to sacrifice other time coins.

Similarly, when Elon Musk opened his SpaceX factory, reporter Scott Pelly from 60 Minutes asked him where his personal desk was. Musk pointed at a simple table, which seemed lost in the middle of the factory with no walls, closets, doors or pictures to enclose or decorate it. Surprised, Pelly asked, "is this really your desk?"

---

17. Brad Stone, *The Everything Store: Jeff Bezos* and the Age of Amazon (New York: Back Bay Books, 2014).

"Yes," answered Musk, "the best money can buy at IKEA." Both Bezos' and Musk's desks were set up almost instantly without wasting many time coins on selection, design, or transportation and without any financial outlay.

Many things can be said about highly successful individuals, but one thing is sure: If they are successful, they are likely to be using their time effectively and efficiently—focusing most of their time on one key valuable time coin and avoiding spending "too much" time on other things—if not for a lifetime, then for some critical period of time required to generate the success they are after.

Take two other serially successful individuals: Mark Zuckerberg and Warren Buffett. They both drove modest cars for many years. One almost always wears the same t-shirt, and the other kept living in the same home he'd owned for decades. These behaviors may be seen as superficial quirks, but it would be a mistake to see them as mere personal preferences. Rather, they are indications of a comprehensive worldview, a perspective that enables Buffett and Zuckerberg to accumulate and create more and more time coins. This perspective allows them to keep acquiring valuable time coins until they reach a critical mass that secures their success, without being swept up in life's endless distractions.

A closer look would likely reveal more examples of the time-oriented lenses through which people like Warren Buffet see the world. We might discover that Buffett didn't own a smartphone until 2020.[18] For anyone living in the 21st century, it's easy to estimate how much time we could save by saying no to smartphones. Nor does Buffett use email, waste time regretting past decisions, or managing a demanding ego.

---

18. Brett Molina, "After years of owning a flip phone, Warren Buffett finally has an iPhone," *USA TODAY*, February 25, 2020.

A readiness to forsake so many types of time coins and focus on truly valuable investments isn't limited to the rich and famous, nor to scientists and entrepreneurs. Many successful people deprioritize their careers, the pressing demands of modern life or excessive consumerism to invest in education, their family, or contributing to society. But these activities are not exempt from the perspective we have discussed so far. The cost of their achievements is giving up many other things, from bragging rights and capital accumulation to influence and power. For some, this is no great loss, whereas others would experience this as a real sacrifice. Some invest more than others in their path to success, while others invest with great effectiveness. But the most successful people likely do both. They effectively invest a significant amount of time coins creating even more or higher-quality ones.

THE LION'S SHARE

The habit of focusing the lion's share of one's time and effort on the most efficient investment lies at the basis of so many success stories and to such an extent that it's difficult to find any successful individual whose behavior doesn't reflect the overwhelming importance they ascribe to a given time coin and their willingness to sacrifice almost any other coin for it.

Should we stumble upon a successful individual who has clearly taken the time to comb his hair and who is wearing matching socks, they are not an exception to this rule. We simply don't know them well enough. They are sacrificing something else.

Bill Gates, for example recounted in an interview how he decided to give up something that, for many of us, is more valuable than haircuts, furniture, shirts or meals. He gave up television. He only persisted in his television abstinence for five years, but five TV-free years represents huge time savings.[19]

Such choices are hardly unique. Pablo Sarasate, a famous musician and composer, once said, "for thirty-seven years I played fourteen hours a day, and now they call me a genius."[20] Thomas Edison, one of the greatest inventors of all times, said that the secret of his success was that he worked eighteen hours a day for 45 years.[21] Marie Curie said "the secret to success? Do not hurry."[22]

Paragons of success don't spend much time on any time coin other than the one that makes them successful, or time coins that prepare them for success.

And although this strategy may seem extreme and might not fit everyone, it's needed to some extent and for some periods of time for each and every one of us. In some cases, there can be no success without it, or at least not at the scale that we would achieve with it. Think of raising a young child, starting a new job, preparing for an exam, or just feeling that you face a once-in-a-lifetime opportunity. This is when we should prioritize the more valuable time coins and deprioritize the less valuable ones.

---

19. Davis Guggenheim, *Inside Bill's Brain*, Netflix, 2021.

20. Shaham, *The Book of Quotations*.

21. Tamar Kochav, *Thomas Edison* (Kinneret, Zmora-Bitan: Or Yehuda, 2010).

22. Shaham, *The Book of Quotations*.

<u>CHAPTER RECAP</u>

- Find a valuable time coin and stick to it.
- Focus means sacrifice too.
- If you aren't the type of person to focus all of your time on one main time coin, that's OK. But remember that we sometimes need to do this anyway, even if just for a little while...
- To achieve greater success, invest a lot and do it effectively over the long run. Make sure you expect to yield a high enough return for yourself and others.
- If you are investing in something that isn't the success you're after, it had better be something that prepares you for the success you'll be pursuing.

PRODUCE LIKE PICASSO
(STRATEGY II)

The previous chapter dealt with people who achieve great success, often serially, by focusing on their one "ace" time coin. This chapter will examine a strategy we call "Produce like Picasso." As the title suggests, the strategy involves finding ways to scale up time-coin production, sometimes to an almost "superhuman" level.

Picasso died at ninety-one, having produced an estimated 13,500 paintings and sketches.[23] Having studied professional painting with his father from age seven to thirteen, he began painting at an early age. And given that he painted professionally for some seventy years, he only needed to paint a little more than one painting every other day to reach his impressive output. Demanding, but not impossible.

However, Picasso's productive output also included 100,000 prints and etchings (four a day), as well as 34,000 illustrations for books and 300 sculptures and ceramic works.[24]

If we want to compete with Picasso for the title of the most productive painter ever, or break records of production in the field of our choice, we had better be careful.[25] Devoting most of our ninety-one years of life to painting (or any other field) will probably not suffice. To compete with Picasso, or others

---

23. Guinness World Records (London: Guinness World Records, 2004).

24. Guinness.

25. Guinness.

like him, we must know something else about the esteemed painter.

The artist whose output dwarfed the greatest of all time—from Michelangelo and Da Vinci to Van Gogh, Rafael, Rembrandt and Monet—had a secret weapon that any brief glance at one of his paintings reveals. It's not that Picasso was more diligent than Michelangelo or slept less than Monet. It's not even the fact that he started at an early age. It was the way he painted. Picasso painted differently.

Picasso was one of the first painters of modern art. Prior to the invention of photography, one of the main goals of art was to achieve complete similitude to reality. But after photography, that goal, in which artists had previously invested countless hours, became pointless and outdated. At least for modern artists like Picasso.[26] Unlike Da Vinci and Michelangelo, Picasso didn't need to invest years, months, weeks or even days in every piece. Nor did he think it was important for his paintings to cover the entire ceiling of the Sistine Chapel. He certainly didn't think he needed to spend much time autopsying human corpses or horses and meticulously sketching every muscle, tendon, and blood vessel simply to achieve a near perfect copy of reality. Instead, Picasso produced more artwork in less time.

---

26. Osip Brik, "Photography versus painting".

ONE RULE FOR ART, SCIENCE
AND EVERYTHING ELSE

Art is not the only field where such unprecedented output has been achieved. Instead of investing decades in experiments, research, and data analysis, Albert Einstein astounded the world by publishing four papers in the world's most prestigious physics journal in a single miraculous year, while holding a junior position in the Swiss Patent Office. How could anyone achieve such unbelievable success in so little time?

Einstein, like Picasso, didn't require as much time as other researchers. Instead of spending his time on meticulous measurements and analyses of the ocean of information in all of reality's aspects and hues, Einstein dealt with a different type of science: Theoretical physics. This was how he could determine, in a split second of thought, that just as gravity attracts celestial bodies, it also attracts light particles (photons). Therefore, a straight beam of light passing near a star must bend slightly, its photons affected by the star's gravity. Einstein, it seems, reached this insight without devoting much more than a fraction of a second to the matter. He then invested the minimal amount of time needed to prove his assumption mathematically. But he didn't spend time validating his theorem. He left the "realistic painting" of the proof to other people. Producing this "painting," which captured the bent light beam by telescopic photography during an eclipse, took four years.

For Einstein, the insight and its mathematical proof sufficed.27 He didn't have to invest time in a journey to Crimea or in trying to explain to the Tsar's officers why he traveled with

---

27. Walter Isaacson, *Einstein: His Life and Universe* (New York: Simon & Schuster, 2008).

advanced observational equipment. Unlike the observers who sought to prove his theorem, Einstein wasn't imprisoned by tsarist officers. Einstein had a more efficient method. Einstein was the Picasso of science.

Even the way in which Picasso and Einstein communicated may be indicative of a similarity that testifies to this common thread. They were both known for their razor-sharp wit. They were both pacifists. Einstein's saying about the future of humanity continues to reverberate in the minds of world leaders and many citizens of the world: "I know not with what weapons World War III will be fought, but World War IV will be fought with sticks and stones."28 It may very well be that his saying is worth a great deal of time coins to us all, perhaps all the time coins we will ever have.

Picasso, too, was a master of effective communications. He created works that were, instead of a perfect reflection of visual reality, transmissions of ideas he chose to make accessible in ways no less creative and effective than the works themselves. During the Spanish Civil War, after the Nazis bombed a Spanish town, killing more than 1,600 people and wounding thousands, Picasso painted "Guernica," depicting the horrors of war, bodies of animals and human beings, their limbs strewn together. When asked by the Nazis, "Did you do this?" Picasso replied: "No, you did."29

---

28. Alice Calaprice, *The Quotable Einstein* (Liberal Judaism magazine, April-May, 1949).

29. Toby Saul, "The horrible inspiration behind one of Picasso's great works," *National Geographic*, May 8, 2018.

INVENTION WITH A TWIST

Picasso didn't need to paint twenty hours a day or avoid human contact, and we don't either. Like Picasso, we can invest time in family life, community involvement and even politics. But we can only scale our success to such heights (and leave enough time for other things) if we find a way to create value as rapidly and effectively as Picasso did.

THINKING DIFFERENTLY

As for the value of Picasso's work, aside from its artistic value, it has garnered some of the highest prices of any works of art ever sold. The total worth of his oeuvre is estimated at nearly a billion dollars. Even if Picasso had printed a dollar bill every three seconds from the day he was born, he could not have made a billion dollars. Nonetheless, not everyone appreciates Picasso's work. Some might not even recognize modern art as a valid form of art.

The real question for our purposes, however, is not how we judge the aesthetic value of Picasso's oeuvre, his artistic style or even his opinions. The real value in this story lies in the answer to the following question: What was the true key to Picasso's success?

After all, not all of us are interested in becoming artists or spending most of our day painting. But if there is a "magic" that allowed not just Picasso, but also Einstein, to achieve greatness in completely different fields, then maybe we could access that magic too, and use it to succeed in any field we like.

So what is the nature of this "magic?" We can sum it up as follows: While we all tend to think of a painting, a scientific proof, a store, a phone, a transportation vehicle, drugs and even a business or a relationship within the limits of our familiar accessible thoughts, they are all essentially means to protect, gain or improve our time. And though it's not the obvious or natural way of thinking, by wrestling with the question "how can we generate more valuable time coins while investing less or better enjoying our investment?" we may have a fair chance of doing things differently. Inventing a new way that redefines efficiency and effectiveness and scales up our production rate and success.

Einstein's and Picasso's paths were revolutionary because they differed from obvious ones. They invested their time in a manner that allowed them to make a greater impact in a shorter period of time. Their paths scaled up their success to unprecedented magnitudes. To do so, they used a way which we will call the timeful way.

And as we focus on our field of choice, we too might benefit from pondering how to reinvent it and choose whether to do things the conventional way or take a precious moment to rethink time, success and the way we are about to get them.

CHAPTER RECAP

- We all work towards gaining what we see as valuable, but stopping to consider a different, more effective way of doing things might be the most valuable thing we can do.
- The key challenge in scaling up our effectiveness is the need to invent—adopt some new approach, thought or perspective—one that is beyond our current reach.

CAPITALIZE LIKE FRANKLIN
(STRATEGY III)

Picasso and Einstein invested most of their time in a single field. We, on the other hand, might not be interested in doing that—either because we don't have a favorite field or because we haven't yet found it. In this case, there is probably no one better to learn from than a truly successful master of all trades—a person who didn't limit himself to any single field, someone who is not a famous painter, author, politician, or scientist, but a completely different kind of individual, one who is successful at everything. A polymath who, instead of sticking to one main type of time coin like Picasso and Einstein, also found success laterally, in every imaginable field. Someone who capitalized on time itself.

LESS IS MORE?
WELL, NOT NECESSARILY

Benjamin Franklin's rise from nothing to everything seems incomprehensible at first glance. Fortunately, Franklin himself explained the reasons for his success and did so in great detail in a four-volume autobiography.

Like many remarkable people who preceded him, Franklin condensed his principles into a single rule. The simple, sharp and catchy expression that has survived for generations and spread across oceans. It remains as relevant today as it was in Franklin's days: Time is money.

Now let's not make the mistake of interpreting Franklin too literally. Franklin clarified in additional sayings that time is more than money. Time is life itself.

Franklin began his path to phenomenal success with only four years of formal schooling. From there, much like Picasso, Franklin hurried to the next stage, devouring every book that passed through his brother's printing house, where he worked as a child. His work there was no coincidence. It would only be fair to emphasize that Franklin ran away from his work at his parents' soap factory. In other words, Franklin too demonstrated "a keen scent" for where the time coins were (or at least to where they weren't for him...). Special access to such a vast treasury of human knowledge, as well as his experience writing a column for his brother's newspaper, led to his mastery of reading, writing, and the use of oral and written knowledge. In other words, he developed outstanding communication skills.

Having developed his communication and printing skills, Franklin published a useful tool with obvious value: A calendar. But Franklin's calendar, known as an Almanac, was unlike anything the world had ever seen. For thousands of years, calendars resembled Leonardo's paintings more than Picasso's art or Einstein's scientific elegance. These older calendars comprised much human knowledge, describing not only the days and the months, but also the movements of celestial bodies, sunsets, astronomical events such as eclipses, and even astrological predictions. They included everything that seemed to matter in the world except for the thing that matters most: Knowledge that could provide us with a bounty of time coins. A kind of knowledge we call wisdom.

Franklin imbued his calendar with this wisdom. But how can a calendar transmit wisdom? Did Franklin reinvent calendars the way Picasso and Einstein revolutionized painting and science? After all, the calendar must represent months and days, holidays and special occasions. Where exactly could Franklin squeeze in all the wisdom he had acquired from the endless books he'd consumed?

Franklin's solution was remarkably similar to Picasso's and Einstein's elegant methods. He decorated the almanac with a handful of brief, catchy and visual messages relating to everyday life: Pearls of wisdom that, when repeated over generations by enough people, are called proverbs.

The quantity of time coins Franklin generated is incalculable. Not only did his almanac become a bestseller, second only to the Bible at the time, it infused the minds of New World settlers with his wisdom for twenty-five consecutive years. If the message was not absorbed in 1732, it got through in 1758. If not to the father or mother, then to the son or daughter.

Upon this impressive success, Franklin built yet another. Should some portion of the wisdom he sought to provide elude a reader in a given year, Franklin stepped in to fill the void. There was no need to purchase all twenty-five of Franklin's almanacs and sift through the old and new pearls that had been published over the years. Franklin spared us our time, collecting and abridging prior ideas in a summary. He wove them into one of the most powerful time coins generators. A catchy story distilling a powerful moral and a no less powerful title.

Franklin published his summary of his twenty-five almanacs' wisdom in The Way to Wealth. The pocketbook rapidly became a bestseller, was translated in Franklin's own lifetime into dozens of languages and remains relevant and sought after to this day. Had we lived in the Thirteen Colonies, Franklin's pearls of wisdom that encouraged us to work diligently, exercise self-discipline and use our time wisely would have earned most of us far more time coins than Newton's first law, Einstein's proofs, the ideas Picasso expressed in his paintings, and even those that Jesus, Buddha, or Lao Tzu expressed in their teachings. And rightly so, for Franklin never sought to share his own wisdom with us. He merely sought to save us thousands of hours of reading, as well as the effort to convert millennia-old parables and examples into contemporary modern life. It is the same thing you'll see all serially successful people in this book do—investing some time and generating more time or perceived quality of time for others.

Franklin even sought to spare us the time and effort required to remember this wisdom by peppering it with humor and rhyme, making it much easier to remember. As he put it, "Not a tenth part of the wisdom was my own, but rather the gleanings I had made of the sense of all ages and nations."30 Franklin thus saved millions of people thousands of days necessary to read the teachings of thinkers from whom he'd gleaned his wisdom. He supplied them with the bottom line and made much useful wisdom accessible, memorable and easy to implement. In fact, what Franklin did was shape human thought. But it is not just some part of human thought that he helped shape. Franklin shaped the part that people were using frequently, on a daily basis. Franklin helped shape what we earlier referred to as "accessible thoughts"—the thoughts we use the most.

---

30. Benjamin Franklin, *The Way to Wealth (Gildan Media, New York, 2007).*

WHAT UNITES THE
SERIALLY SUCCESSFUL

The importance of time and its effective management didn't diminish with the years. In January 2004, Michelle Singletary, President of the Washington Post's "Color of Money Book Club," named Franklin's book its title of the month. She explained in short: "This thirty-page long pocketbook enables the acquisition of the financial wisdom of an entire lifetime in less than an hour."

Franklin also helped draft the American Declaration of Independence, established the world's first lending library, founded a major university, started a club for entrepreneurs, and saved many from death by lightning by inventing the lightning rod. And that's not to mention inventing a more efficient wood-burning stove, lecturing on the evils of overeating, improving Philadelphia's streets with flagstones, and inventing the bifocal lenses.

So, is there a common denominator in Franklin's work? Some secret connecting all his inventions and efforts?

Why did Franklin not limit himself, like so many other successful individuals, to a significant and meaningful contribution in a single field? Did the man who invented the English word "battery," the phrases "positive and negative poles," and the grounding device lack sufficient skills to make additional contributions to that field? Would it not have been better to focus solely on diplomacy and statecraft? If he saw and presented himself, in spite of all his other accomplishments, primarily as a publisher and printer of books, then why didn't Franklin invest all of his time in publishing and print? Or did he?

The heating stove, the sidewalk, bifocal lenses and the lightning rod can, of course, be seen as separate and unrelated inventions in completely different fields (thermodynamics, civil engineering, optics and electrical engineering). But there's another way to look at these separate fields. They can all be seen as tools that help us save, gain, improve or trade our time. Tools that grant us and others what we perceive to be a better life, or at least a few preferable time coins. If Franklin saw the world in such a manner, maybe he didn't recognize a difference between a sidewalk, a heating stove, bifocal lenses, an almanac and a lightning rod. Perhaps he saw no difference between a joke, a rhyme, a respectful attitude to others, diplomacy, adopting a useful habit, and avoiding offensive actions one might later regret. In fact, Franklin may well have looked at the world and seen nothing but a single ubiquitous currency: Time coins.

This perspective would have revealed to him a very different and simpler world than what most of us experience. He would have seen a world in which the complexities of our society, culture, religion, and even our own conflicts aren't so complex after all. From this perspective, Franklin's willingness to serve as Ambassador of the United States to France as well as Postmaster General, while also collecting and buying filthy rags and paper scraps that he sold for recycling and impersonating a pious widow writing a column in a newspaper, seems more understandable. After all, what does it matter if it was all the same in Franklin's world? They were all different names and different ways for producing and trading time coins in the most effective way possible. It may be that Franklin truly didn't see himself as a scientist, a statesman, an inventor, a publisher, a writer, an educator or even a polymath. To him, they were all the same.

PRINTING TIME COINS

From age seventeen to eighty-four, Franklin presented himself as a printer, regardless of the post he held. But perhaps this reveals only half of his secret to success. For Franklin was indeed a printer. He printed books, bills, newspapers, almanacs, and even new time-saving habits he sought to adopt and share with others. He also "printed" non-human time-savers, from a coal stove and a chimney to lightning rods and lenses. Franklin was indeed a printer, but not a printer of books. For Franklin was a printer of time coins.

That leads us to an important question:
What are you going to "print?"

If you find something to be as valuable as one of Franklin's creations, something that others can "print" or join forces with you in an effective collaboration, please share it using #timefulness #timeprinting, or #printlikefranklin.

CHAPTER RECAP

- Everything we do is an effort to save, protect, gain or improve our time.
- Time is money. More importantly—it's your life too.
- We all think in terms of labels. Such labels represent a value we think highly of—we are a polymath, a business leader, a publisher, inventors, etc. But it's not how we call ourselves that matters the most, but the amount and quality of time we create.
- Focusing on the more valuable time coins allows us more easily to drop a task for a more promising one.
- Seeking time coins is not an excuse to avoid completing valuable projects (such as publishing almanacs for 25 years). It's a systematic way to continuously focus on what matters most and leverage it to create more value (like weaving the almanacs into a comprehensive story and publishing it as a book).
- One way to leverage success is to make valuable time coins easily accessible to others—ideally many others.
- The most valuable thing you can do is to positively influence the public's accessible thoughts.

LEAD LIKE SCHWAB
(STRATEGY IV)

Getting back to Emily, the insightful young woman who toyed with the idea of closing the gap between her and Einstein in more than just socks. She just started a new job and one month into it, she got back from the ICU where, as the company's product manager, she provides support for a new drug delivery system, an electronic infusion pump.

She saw her boss in the corridor and went straight up to him. "The pump keeps beeping," she exclaims. "There are tons of problems. The medical teams are unhappy and keep getting stuck with the operation of the device. As a result, they switch to competitors' devices, and we can't accumulate the log hours we need to learn and improve." Emily ranted for a whole minute. Once she'd finished, Shaul, her manager, asked with surprising empathy, "Emily, what are you concerned about?"

Emily was not sure what to do. She actually thought she'd gone too far with the venting and that she'd probably be scolded at the end of it. It was as if Shaul hadn't listened to what she said, but only to her tone of voice. A tone saying only one thing: Emily is concerned about something important. But what is that important thing? Emily covered it up with so many words that no one could understand what it was—not even Emily herself.

She had to stop and think it through. Shaul waited patiently. "Look," she said eventually, "I'm doing a lot of stuff at the office, and I'm in the ICU supporting the system only after office hours and during weekends. The morning shift disconnects our pumps if no one is there to solve whatever needs solving. When I get back in the evening, it might take me four hours of waiting just to get a few minutes with a nurse or a doctor to walk them through the process and convince them to switch back to our pump—since we are in the evaluation phase. If I could just be there when the pump was beeping during the morning shift, I would explain and solve it on the spot and not have to wait four hours to get it going again."

"I see," said Shaul. "So why are you at the office?" he asked with an invisible smile.

Emily smiled too in her heart, turned away, and realized there were only a few more weeks of evaluation, and nothing is more important than succeeding there. Every hour counts! Every second is critical! Worrying about the office (including about what people would think if she weren't there) isn't going to help anyone.

"Oh, and Emily," added Shaul as she walked away. "Take everyone in the company—and I mean everyone, no matter how senior—and sign them up for shifts in the ICU whenever you're not there."

Wow, what a shift in the path to success, thought Emily, as she sat in a quarterly meeting a few weeks later. Just when the CEO called her name, gave her an envelope with a check, and thanked her in front of the company's fifty employees for gaining 10,000 log hours instead of the ambitious 4,000 that was her goal. Emily thanked her coworkers who helped manage her shifts and Shaul, who helped her gain so much timefulness with just a little mindfulness.

TO LEAD IS TO BECOME

Emily's ICU incident is proof that we don't need to be a Picasso or Einstein to work magic in our own lives. We don't even need to be a Shaul or Emily. It's enough to open our mind, heart or ears and follow our governing principle towards a more timeful life.

Many of us enjoy a wealth of possibilities beyond our needs and even our ability to grasp them. If we ask ourselves what we truly want above all else in life, many will earnestly answer that health is the most important thing. Others will say that nothing beats being happy or helping others. But whatever the answer might be, within a few seconds we'll find ourselves struggling to fulfill half a dozen conflicting ambitions. The ability to focus on a single desire or goal can greatly increase our chances of success. And if there's one thing we have learned we should focus on, it's to act in a timeful manner. It can be one valuable "coin" or another, one or a few that we pursue, but we have to be timeful—it has to be something we'll do in a way that will allow us to work the magic of time— to pour in some time coins in the form of time, thought, effort or budget and use them to create more or better time coins— effectively protecting or increasing time-coin wealth (ours or that of others).

###

When we repeat timeful choices, the greatest magic of all happens—we become ever more timeful and inspire others to become timeful too. Use #timefulness #toleadistobecome to share your stories of how you took a timeful decision, became timeful or lead an important initiative in a timeful manner.

A TIMEFUL CHALLENGE

Emily recalls another person who demonstrated such timeful-ness, her colleague Andrei Yosef. An otherwise ordinary per-son transformed by life's circumstances into an industrious and highly self-disciplined individual. However, like many others, he still used "human" expressions such as "not pos-sible" and "we can't do that in time." But over time, things changed. After several months working together, Emily sat next to him in a company meeting. Over an entire hour Andrei explained that he lacked resources, employees, time and bud-gets to get the job done. He concluded by stating that the sit-uation was impossible and that he required urgent aid. The planning session ended, and everyone began to discuss chal-lenging technological bottlenecks of the type that had previ-ously brought the company to bankruptcy. Towards the end of the meeting, Dr. Boaz Eitan, the new CEO who'd recently purchased the bankrupt company, turned to Andrei, who had yet to catch his breath from his hour-long tirade on resource shortages. Dr. Eitan made clear that there was no choice but to find a solution to a problem that had so far been considered impossible to solve. He told Andrei, "This needs to be solved within a week. Can you do it?" Emily's colleague didn't hesi-tate before he answered with a confident "yes." Everyone was stunned. The CEO asked, "You said you lacked people, resourc-es, budgets. How can you be certain you'll solve the problem?" Andrei shrugged. "You said there's no choice." And with that, the meeting ended.

It may have been the shortest meeting Emily ever attend-ed. Within three days, it turned out that it had also been the most effective. Emily stared at her colleague in wonder as he put aside all emotions, frustrations, and doubts and simply did what needed to be done. Within a few years, this good friend, who back then managed only one employee, managed a division of 200. A short time thereafter, Andrei became CEO of a subsidiary of Eitan's Group—Sorrel Medical, sold for more than $100 million during 2023.[31]

Solving problems and managing employees wasn't, of course, the only thing Andrei could do by focusing and controlling his thoughts and emotions. Over two years, Emily and Andrei played tennis together. He always won. He was never discouraged when he missed and didn't lose focus when he won. They continued to play until, well, I guess you can guess until when... Emily and Andrei continued playing tennis until he moved to a different city. In other words, until it cost him too much time...

This is not, however, an anecdote about one person or a special case. Since Emily's youth, she recalls how her father would recount to her how he'd earned a significant promotion. His workplace also had a challenge to solve, this challenge was also discussed in a meeting, and their CEO also assigned resolution of the challenge to one of his employees, in this case Emily's father. A senior executive approached him after the meeting and asked whether he really knew how to solve the problem. "I have no clue," Emily's father replied.

"What then will you do?" asked the manager.

"Find a solution," replied Emily's father. The senior executive smiled, turned around, and walked away.

Time was precious. It still is.

31. Gali Weinreb, "The High-Tech Pilot Who Reinvented Himself: The Medical Device Exit of Boaz Eitan," Globes, June 20, 2023, https://www.globes.co.il/news/article.aspx?did=1001449811.

TIMEFUL PERSPECTIVE—TIMEFUL RESULTS

One famous example of the ability to choose a timeful response is Charles Schwab, Andrew Carnegie's favorite employee, more than a hundred years ago. Schwab arrived to inspect one of Carnegie's steel factories—the company's poorest functioning steel mill. The workers were nervous about his visit. Their former colleague had become the right-hand man of the sensational international steel magnate. Schwab looked at the factory's morning shift, asked one brief question, scribbled something on the floor, and disappeared.

Rumors of Schwab's surprise inspection circulated among the workers and became the talk of the day. But there was not, in fact, much to say. The men asked about the purpose of his visit, but it was brief. All that the night-shift workers who arrived to replace their morning-shift colleagues were able to find out was that Mr. Schwab asked about the number of steel rods produced during the shift and wrote the number— six—on the floor with a piece of chalk. The night shift workers couldn't believe it. Wasn't he angry? Didn't he ask anything else? Nothing, was the answer. He came, he wrote, he left.

The night shift ended up being more efficient. When it ended, the proud workers scrawled their output—seven—on the factory floor. The morning shift erased that number and proudly wrote ten down instead. Within days, the factory with the lowest output in Carnegie's steel mill conglomerate became the most productive steel mill worldwide.[32] Schwab's brief visit was a stunning success. It's no wonder that Schwab was the first salaried employee on our planet to earn more

---

32. Dale Carnegie, *How to Win Friends & Influence People*, Simon & Schuster Audio, New York, 2004, Napoleon Hill, *The Wisdom of Success: The Philosophy of Achievement by Andrew Carnegie & Napoleon Hill*, Wisdom of Success, 2014.

than a million dollars a year. What Schwab could achieve in a few minutes, many couldn't achieve in a lifetime. At least, not without a timeful perspective—the perspective of a truly great leader.

Use #timefulleader to share examples of timeful leaders you admire—take part in setting the standard we deserve.

CHAPTER RECAP

- We can gain much timefulness with just a little mindfulness.
- When opportunity calls, say YES to the timefulness challenge.
- If fear and inhibitions stop you from taking on a challenge, ask yourself if you are in real danger, or if you are actually facing an opportunity to profit in exchange for a risk you are willing to take.
- To lead is to become: Become timeful and people will follow.
- Finding an effective way to deal with life's challenges is not easy, but with the right perspective, it's not so difficult either.

ENVISION LIKE MUSK
(STRATEGY V)

Some serially successful people choose to invest in one or more existing sources of time coins, while others envision new ones. After all, why pursue an existing time coin, as valuable as it may be, if you can create a more valuable one?

Such visionaries can see in their mind's eye the vehicles or computers of the future, or the life we may live in a hundred years. They might insist on the utmost importance of designing a new computer so that the processor and the screen are assembled as a single unit. They can seem obsessed with seemingly inconsequential details that they alone know are vital to fulfilling their vision. But why is that? And what kind of details do they obsess over?

Take a computer handle. A visionary might proclaim that a computer handle must be cast in a single mold with the computer case. Otherwise, this now "handle focused" visionary (Steve Jobs) passionately argues, customers unpacking their new computer, might feel alienated from it. Unless the handle is made an inseparable part of the computer, it will fail to bridge between man and machine.[33] The magic will fail, and we'll all stay mired in the past.

It's hard not to conclude that Steve Jobs was indeed a sort of a magician, capable of creating products and symbols that inspired near religious zeal in people. But was he really a wizard? Or is there something else we are missing?

33. Isaacson, *Steve Jobs*.

Perhaps this is a rare case of worshiping Steve Jobs himself and not his creations? But what about other examples? What about Elon Musk, whose Tesla vehicle handle almost became the straw that broke the back of the company's engineers?

Fixating on a computer or car door handle and transforming it into a mythological object with almost religious significance may seem like even more than a flash of brilliance. Even when it works, we find it hard to believe it's really just the handle. We're not idiots, after all. Why would a handle lead anyone to buy a $100,000 car? But Musk is no dupe either. So maybe there really is something magical that only true visionaries can see when they think about handles, something that the rest of us miss. And maybe this isn't a magic trick reserved for a few elite magicians. Maybe we can all look at the handle and see something else. Maybe at some point, deep in our minds, we can look out on the world and see time.

SEE THE MAGIC FOR WHAT IT IS

As with all great magic tricks, the secret isn't in what catches the eye, but what doesn't. People who look at a Tesla or an Apple product and believe its success lies in design details have fallen prey to an illusion.

When we open a computer package and something tells us lift me out of here in a gentle and natural manner, we feel good about ourselves. We sense that we bought the right product and won't be missing out on other, better options. We feel the pleasant tingle of success and freedom from doubts. We will feel that we did a good job and lost no time coins. The sensation of time loss we expected during the unpacking was in fact converted into a different feeling—a feeling of winning time-coin wealth. Even if the profit is as brief as a split second, its quality makes that coin dear to us.

The Tesla's retractable handles are magical in the same way that the iMac handle was. They not only make the vehicle more aerodynamic, faster, and more efficient, but transform the time spent on using them into a pleasant experience. You still need to pull the handle, but it gives you a glimpse of a handle-free future. It shows us the car is going the extra mile.

The handle transforms formerly unpleasant time coins into time we can enjoy. Even when we tire of the time-shifting magic of the handles, we can always find someone new to impress with this "trick" and efficiently convert the time coins we've spent into valuable coins of social recognition.

Perhaps in one respect, little has changed since the days we told stories about mythological apples. If we can excite or impress others sufficiently with either a painting, scientific discovery, a handle or some story, we are in fact creating great value, or at least many will feel this way.

Companies like Apple and Tesla that pour significant resources into design aren't investing in computer or car design. They're investing in the design of human time. Musk and Jobs are more architects than CEOs. Not architects of designs that succeed due to our fondness for handles or the color white, but time wizards, who succeed because we love positive time coins.

If you still suspect that some factor other than the basic building blocks of time must underlie the successes we describe here, you can hardly be blamed. Most of us are so deeply committed to other lenses, whether "coolness" or technical jargon, it can be hard to get on the "time" beam and stay there.

Where we see items, goods and services as discrete categories, the great visionaries see them all, consciously or not, as just units of time. Some go so far as to count and calculate the number of seconds they could save. Thus, while we think of them as product designers, architects, inventors or CEOs, highly successful individuals are actually efficient time wizards who are not intimidated by the challenge of quantifying the time coins required for an investment as well as the time coins the investment will generate. A calculation that results in the true net value of any human endeavor. And you might already have a fairly good guess of the "crazy" person who will take such an unusual step as counting seconds of one product version versus another.

The following story may best exemplify how such successful individuals implement the principles of a timefulness vision in their work. The story took place when Steve Jobs approached Larry Kenyon, the engineer charged with designing the Macintosh operating system, and asked him to cut down its booting time. Kenyon didn't think boot time was a significant issue. In fact, he had plenty of other work on his hands. The product launch was imminent, and perhaps he even had some personal or social desires he wanted to invest in after work hours. Besides, everyone knows that computers take time to boot. It didn't seem reasonable to sacrifice a family evening or postpone handling a severe software malfunction for minutiae that would only save a few seconds. But Jobs was relentless. In his pursuit of faster boot times, he exposed the real secret behind one of the most successful companies in the world: The magic of time. It is the ability of just one single person or a group to invest X amount of time and save or better much more than that for many others. Jobs explained that if fifty million computers were sold and each computer would save only ten seconds every day, this saving would amount to about 50,000 hours a year. Hence, shortening the computer boot process by just ten seconds might save the time equivalent of the total lifespan of almost ten people. Every single year. The engineer said he would see what he could do. Kenyon cut boot time not by ten seconds, but by twenty-eight seconds.[34] His family or friends may have been disappointed that he failed to see them for a while, but the twenty-two composite statistical lives he saved during the first year of Macintosh sales alone made the world better for Apple and for many others too.

HOW TO MAKE YOUR VISION
A DISRUPTIVE ONE

Steve Jobs was unique. To many, he was a once-in-a-generation genius. Whether as a technological guru, a visionary or a genuine magician, Jobs led revolutions in at least seven fields, from computing and communications to music, photography and movies. He brought a new and flourishing world of applications into the world of smartphones, all because he understood that the basis for all successes lies in providing time coin value, which he measured by the second, or intuited as minimalism or the arousal of positive feelings. Other serially successful people, companies, governments and different types of organizations get it too. Some are more aware of it while others are less so. Some might follow a century-old family business enheartened, others stick to their core values, a catchy slogan, or a great product, but dig deeper, and you'll find it's always the same custom in a different disguise. They effectively provide enough people with more or better time coins than the available alternatives—they all perform the magic of time. In other words, they act timefully. This "magic of time" can

---

34. Isaacson, Steve Jobs.

shine so brightly, that we would find it hard to resist. It would become an irresistible vision and source of attraction.

And if we plan on having a successful vision, we had better make it shine. We had better make our timeful creation one that can increase people's time-coin wealth significantly enough compared with the alternatives.[35] An opportunity that our governing principle will find so compelling, it will tilt the global flow of time coins and time-coin wealth—a tilt we call "disruption."

If you have such a vision in mind, use #timefulness #timefulvision #envisionlikemusk to share your idea with our evolving timeful community.

BECOMING TIMEFUL—BECOMING A SUCCESS

"I might have a big vision someday," thinks Emily, "but in the meantime, how can I put timefulness to work in my everyday life here and now?"

Emily tries to think of someone more approachable than CEOs of big companies or Nobel Laureates. Someone she knows from her own life experiences. Someone she can more easily relate to. In fact, it's someone we all know from our own life. But it's not just some one, it's two different people. The person we like and the person we don't.

---

35. Based on Tversky and Kahneman's findings, an average of 2.5 higher profit in total time coins compared with the alternatives would be a good place to start.

Let's call the first Dan and the second Zik.[36] Dan is the person who has time for you whenever you want to see him. If he doesn't, he will find the time anyhow and won't tell you about it. As soon as you suggest a date and time, it's a done deal. If something comes up, and you can't make it—it's alright. When he senses you might need a favor, he kindly asks you to give him the honor, before you have to ask. Sometimes even when you only think of calling him, he calls you.

In other words, when he's around, so are the positive time coins—jokes, laughter, good moods, insights and valuable life advice. There's no complexity, anger or embarrassment when he's around. Just a good positive flow of time—life as we all want it.

Unfortunately, not all our friends are like Dan. One of them is called Zik—and he's a pest. Every time he calls, the call lasts an hour, and it wouldn't matter if you told him you were on your way out the door. At the end of the hour, you feel your brain has turned to mush. You'll need a long night's sleep to recover.

Zik is easily offended. Scheduling a meeting with him is a complicated never-ending project, and speaking your mind to him can be very costly. Any interaction with Zik will cost you precious time coins and gain you none.

Most of us have met a few Ziks along the way. But if we're honest, we'll probably admit to having a little Zik right inside us too, along with a good deal of Dan. The fact is, each and every one of us has some of Zik and some of Dan in us. We can all err occasionally by not listening, making a mistake in our timing or interrupting someone's train of thought. It's hard to imagine a person who's never insulted, had bad timing, or responded inappropriately. Yet some of us manage to provide

---

36. Randomly chosen names.

ourselves and those around us with many valuable time coins. Frequently, more than many others do. And Emily's idea of becoming a time wizard in this sense, in her everyday life, is a good plan that's sure to lead to success.

Even without starting a company that will change the world or working at one—or perhaps even only until she does—Emily will hold on to her idea of becoming just a little more like Dan and a little less like Zik.

She'll plan her actions to better respect other people's time, protect it, or help them gain more or better time. She'll enable others to enjoy a greater time-coin wealth when she is around. Whether by means of a compliment, a gesture, a smile, or perhaps even by "infecting" one of her friends with the concept of timefulness. And if not that, then just listening, showing empathy or taking a genuine interest in them—the things we all value and sometimes give too little of, as we are busy gaining time coins rather than giving them to others.

And if Emily can do that—constantly rejecting "opportunities" to harm people's time with criticism, arguments, disrespect, and other negative time coins, and instead become an everlasting source of positive time coins wherever she goes, will she not become her own brand of serial success?

CHAPTER RECAP

- A vision is an idea for a new source of time coins or a different way to produce time coins from an existing source.
- While we all pursue existing sources of time coins, we can also invent new ones.
- New sources of time coins can allow us to work the magic of time—to invest X amount of time and save or better it for ourselves or others.
- Some of the most impressive visions are those that generate a significant shift in our feelings about and usage of time. They devise solutions that remove the pain or the non-satisfying and provide pleasure instead. They create enjoyable and rewarding time coins.
- An irresistible vision is one that creates a new or a different source of time coins—one that is so much more attractive than existing alternatives, that it can tilt the global flow of time coins—a phenomenon known as disruption.
- Every interaction in our life is an opportunity to make or lose time coins.
- By becoming a source of positive time coins, we are not only becoming better friends, employees, leaders or parents for others, but also better, more timeful people for ourselves.
- A big vision that will tilt the global flow of time coins is one way to success. Minimizing negative time coins and increasing positive ones is another way to go.

FUTURECAST LIKE BUFFETT
(STRATEGY VI)

In the last strategy we examined—Envision, where Steve Jobs and Elon Musk were our guides—the ambitions, the required sacrifice, and the overall stakes were all in the stratosphere. Emily's vision to continuously act timefully is not necessarily easier or simpler. Fortunately, we don't have to be a Jobs, a Musk, or an Emily to achieve great success. An equally powerful strategy is to predict instead of create.

That way doesn't require us to imagine or do the actual work in order to create a new reality. In other words, instead of creating the future, we can simply predict and invest in it.

In some fields, like weather forecasting or specific medical situations, predicting the future is now considered reliable. In some other areas, such predictions seem impossible. Yet there are those who dare to make predictions in even the most perilous fields. One such field is the stock market.

For Warren Buffett, the Oracle of Omaha, it appears as if making predictions is simple and easy. Where investments are concerned, he seems to foresee the future. How else can you explain his consistent record of success over three generations? Despite the occasional failure, there is no disputing that Buffett has excelled at predicting the future. So, how does he do it?

Like other modern successes, the Oracle of Omaha doesn't claim to hold a mystical secret. In fact, he has explained his success time and time again. It turns out that instead of predicting stocks' value, he predicts something much simpler and no less valuable: "The potential that a company will do better at some point in the future."[37] A potential, that in Buffett's eyes, should push the value of securities to a higher level at some unknown point.

Buffett has explained that he doesn't purchase shares, he invests in companies offering a future potential of higher value. Buffett knows it's impossible to predict the value of a given stock at any point in time. There are simply too many variables, far too many for even Einstein to represent in an elegant equation. So instead of trying to determine the value of a stock at a set point in time, Buffett remembers that stocks, securities, share prices—they are smoke and mirrors, and instead chooses to ask a simpler question: Can this company do better in the future?

The difference between predicting the value of a stock within a specific amount of time and investing in the hope that the company will take off one day is a big difference. It's nothing less than the difference between the impossible and the possible. Just like the difference between trying to predict when a seed will sprout and knowing that it will do so when the time comes. Or in the Oracle's own words:

> "Because with stocks, people make decisions every second, they think an investment in stocks is different than an investment in a business. But it isn't. Nobody buys a farm based on whether they think it's going to rain next year. You're buying businesses."[38]

37. Alice Schroeder, *The Snowball: Warren Buffett and the Business of Life*, Random House Audio, New York, 2008.

38. Warren Buffett in a CNBC interview with Emmie Martin, February 24th, 2020.

Buffett buys businesses he intends to own forever, not stocks he intends to sell when they peak. But even if we adopt such a long-term approach, how can we identify which business-es we want to own forever? If you accept that the premise of a business is to generate profit, and that every one of us is seek-ing to better his lot by gaining more time coins, then invest-ing in a business that can efficiently provide a growing num-ber of people with a growing number of time coins seems like a sound guiding principle.[39] If this sounds complicated, the Oracle explained it in simpler words: "I try to invest in busi-nesses that are so wonderful that even an idiot can run [them]. Because sooner or later, one will."

But perhaps more importantly than the fact that any idi-ot can manage a timeful company, is that any idiot can spot one too. At times, Buffett's investment considerations seem embarrassingly simple. So simple they simply must be true.

Buffett once explained that he's in no rush to invest in tech-nology companies because he avoids investing in fields he doesn't understand. In other words, Buffett doesn't invest in futures he can't predict. He explained that he can't know what computers will do five or ten years down the line, but he's fairly certain that the humans sitting in front of the computer screen and punching the keys, regardless of how many hours they work, what programming language they are using, and what software they are coding, will still occasionally snack on a bar.

And if you can't predict it,
perhaps you shouldn't invest in it either...

---

39. This content or any other content in the book is not to be seen as an investments consultancy or advice but is only offered to the reader as a thought-provoking content.

BECOME A PROPHET OF PROFIT

It's true that some of Buffett's investments require more complex decision-making than investing in a tasty snack or a soft drink. But like other successful figures, Buffett relies on simple principles. Like in the case where he changed his mind and invested in Apple only when learning how dear a time coin source the iPhone could be. That happened after his nonagenarian director and friend lost his own iPhone and behaved as if he'd lost himself.[40] This focus of considering investment based on what people grant high value to, enables him not just to make sound predictions, but to generate serial successes by making such predictions time and time again.

Some of you have been fortunate or insightful enough to do extremely well on a given investment or investments, perhaps even throughout a respectable period. You may even ask yourselves with much retrospective wisdom, how could Buffett have missed out on such an obvious investment? The answer is that true prophets don't presume to be all-knowing. They merely predict enough to succeed. Like other serially successful individuals, the great prophets simply have a timeful approach, and a healthy dose of self-discipline that restrains them from rolling the dice one time too many. The "magic" behind what great prophets achieve really boils down to accurately predicting our behaviors and preferences, mostly for time and the value of time.

Just as Jeff Bezos can look into the future and confidently predict that people will always want to make purchases fast-

---

40. Theron Mohamed, *Warren Buffett invested in Apple after learning how upset his friend was about losing his iPhone, a new book says*, Business Insider, May 12, 2022, https://markets.businessinsider.com/news/stocks/warren-buffett-berkshire-hathaway-apple-tech-stock-iphone-taxi-weschler-2022-5.

er, cheaper and from a growing number of options presented effectively,[41] Buffett gazes into the future and confidently
determines that people will consume more Coca-Cola.[42]

Buffett and Bezos are of course examples of incredibly successful figures. But aren't we all prophets of some kind? Don't
we all predict the future some of the time?

Without the ability to predict the future, how would we get
through the day? We might be too fearful even to eat without
having some way of predicting whether the food is safe. We
wouldn't be able to cross the street, for how could we be certain that a car wouldn't pop out of nowhere and hit us? Even
working for a monthly salary or hourly rate would become
impossible, as it would pose too great of a risk of not being
paid. Our ability to predict the future expands our time coin
trade options. This ability enables nothing short of human
progress itself.

Serially successful people can more confidently predict
returns on their investment in the shape of future time coin
gains. Many times, not because of some sophisticated idea, but
due to a simple perspective. This, together with their devotion
to their "ace" time coin, is the key to their success. Free of constant uncertainty, they can commit to their investment until
they succeed. For highly successful individuals, life is some-
what simpler—they predict, they invest and they collect.

41. Jeff Bezos interview for the Internet Association.

42. "Warren Buffett Explains Why You Should Own Food Stocks." *The
Long-Term Investor*. February 25, 2023. Video, https://www.youtube.
com/watch?v=q7yInbYLBX8.

TRANSFORM YOUR LIFE
ONE BOLD STEP AT A TIME

Emily is excited. She has planned a picnic with her sister, Sarah, who hasn't been out much since giving birth to her first son. Emily expects the outing to be fun, and it is. The sun is shining, her four-year-old nephew is running around in the green grass, laughing happily, and very pleased with himself. He sits on the blanket and finishes all the food, which naturally pleases Sarah too. Then, he runs around with his bottle trying to feed the birds and flowers. For "dessert," he falls asleep in his mother's lap, while Emily and Sarah enjoy a relaxed heart-to-heart talk. Sarah then moves her son to his stroller with a loving smile, adding that she thinks he'll sleep for another hour and that she can't remember the last time she'd had such a good long talk. She then straps him in and, with a flick of her wrist, picks up the blanket, which sends dozens of golden-brown crumbs into the air, as the birds chirp with excitement.

It's only then that Emily realizes what has just happened. Why her prediction of quality picnic time has come true. And more importantly, how to repeat this two-hour success.

The whole picnic seemed perfectly normal, she thinks, except for one odd fact. Sarah didn't mind all the crumbs falling from her son's mouth while he was eating. Emily remembered what a disaster his recent fourth birthday party was. Emily, Sarah and her husband, four grandparents and the child, of course, all went out to eat. The stress was visible on Sarah's face. Sarah's husband drove for an hour in traffic while the birthday boy kept crying in the car. The boy missed his nap, and Sarah and her husband got into an argument because he'd stopped and taken a call from the office instead of parking—a move that cost them quite a bit of extra time. Then, at the restaurant, Sarah was constantly worried and embarrassed about Junior's table manners, and she kept collecting his crumbs and cleaning up after him. Just as she'd finished cleaning, he knocked over a glass, which, although small, still created a tsunami across the table. While everyone was picking up glass off the floor, the little angel, now sans diaper, made another mess. Sarah's husband rushed him to the toilet, but on the way back, he hit his head on the table and started howling in pain.

"The picnic was so much better, but why?" Emily wonders. How could she have predicted it? She had a gut feeling, but could she "reverse engineer" it?

Emily closes her eyes and replays the scene where Sarah was waving the blanket and the crumbs were flying into the air. "Now I've got it," Emily thinks. "At the restaurant, every crumb that fell cost Sarah a small-time coin. She felt she needed to find it, pick it up, get rid of it, and wipe off her hands or—even worse—achieve the impossible and find a way to prevent crumbs from falling to begin with. At the restaurant, in other words, Sarah pays dearly in precious time coins for each crumb that falls out of her son's mouth. At the picnic, it's a non-issue. No one is judging the boy's table manners since there is no table. Better still, getting rid of the crumbs doesn't cost her any time. She just pulls up her picnic blanket. Problem solved."

What's more, she doesn't have to worry about her son bumping into anything, spilling stuff, being noisy or stinking up a restaurant. She started on the right foot with a five-minute walk to the park—no car, no car seats, no traffic, no parking or badly timed phone calls. She was as free as can be, with very few concerns, more flow, less risk and far better use of every time coin she had.

Surprisingly, Sarah and her husband made a tradition out of

celebrating their son's birthday at that same restaurant. "Daddy just loves it!" Sarah says. But Emily knows better. Their father once confided to Emily that he thought the whole thing was a big waste of money, but that he hasn't felt comfortable telling Sarah.

And so, the show goes on, except for one little change. Emily has now had an epiphany. She thinks she might be able to plan her life with more "picnic time" and less "daddy's favorite restaurant" time—and she does.

FEASTING ON TIME

Organizing her thoughts, Emily asks what few things in life give her the greatest happiness, meaning and fulfilment. What are the things in her life that are really worth living for. Emily writes her top twenty in her notebook: Deep insights, laughter, positively impacting other people's lives, striving towards worthy goals, living your values, heart-to-heart talks, admiring nature, listening to a new favorite song, food, becoming better version of myself, reading a book or watching TV, playing a favorite game, doing sports and dancing. Then, taking a deep breath that brings more sincerity to her thought, she adds: Love, sex, a good massage, chocolate and very strong coffee.

Emily then writes down her greatest negative time coins:

From dropping and breaking things to going out when her hair isn't quite perfect.

She realizes this might be too much. She has to focus on just one, two or three time coins worth having and a couple to get rid of—preferably with only a flick of her wrist. Otherwise, what kind of time wizard would she be? "Can't I focus on just one or two things?" Emily asks herself.

She eyes the top twenty positive time coins list when she realizes that one single thing could give her most, if not all, of the time coins on her list. She needs the right life partner. Adding to it the right job and a timefulness approach, she could earn all the other time coins by herself.

She now focuses on some of the negative time coins. From waiting for the dryer to finish, to having her apartment look like a messy dorm room because she had a presentation to prepare.

She then thinks of some bigger things she'd like in her life but rarely finds time for: Putting enough time into her career, getting a promotion, finding time to go to the movies, making dinner at home or taking a weekend trek in the countryside.

"Wouldn't a housekeeper solve that?" She thinks. "Wouldn't that allow me to avoid some of my most troubling time coins and take on some of the most challenging investments? I am already saving a modest fifty bucks a week, but my time these days is as precious as it will ever be. This year will probably affect my career more than any other, since it's my first job in the industry. If all I do is go to work and come home to cook and clean, how will I ever get all the other coins I want—finding my second half, putting in extra time at work, or just being happy about coming home to clean sheets on the bed?"

Emily thought her idea to save the occasional ten minutes of folding socks was pretty clever. Some quick calculations, however, made her realize she could save at least six hours every week with a little domestic help.

So Emily hired a housekeeper. Within six months, she was the first and only employee ever to get a raise before the end of her first year at the company, and during a challenging period of pay freezes while the company sought to become solvent. True, the raise was symbolic, only funding a little less than half of what Emily paid her housekeeper. But she could now easily predict what would happen six months down the road—and where it could lead her in the years to come.

Past Emily would never have hired help. She felt that she alone knew how to put her underwear in the drawer. She believed that people need to do their own work and clean up after themselves, that paying others to do what you can do yourself makes very little sense. Besides, the last thing she needed was a stranger in the house making her feel she "couldn't handle it" herself.

"I was stupid," Emily now thinks. But just in case, she schedules housekeeper visits while she's at work. After all, "stupid" feelings also count when you're adding up your time-coin wealth.

CHAPTER RECAP

- No one is born an inventor, entrepreneur, artist or scientist. You can become a person who will invent the future for others, but you can also choose to invest in someone else's success—especially if they are a serially successful person, company, country, or group.
- Making a nonexplicit, long-term prediction could be as valuable to you as making a harder, more explicit one.
- Predicting the future is something we all do to survive and thrive.
- If you can't predict it, you might not want to invest in it either.
- You don't need to predict everything about the future. Just one or a few basic predictions can provide you with all the time-coin wealth you need.
- A good prediction will release us from the constant uncertainty, creating the higher level of commitment needed for our success.
- Plan your life to include more "picnic time" and less "daddy's favorite restaurant" time.
- Make a list of the twenty top positive time coins that can truly make your life better and the twenty negative ones you most wish to avoid.
- Try to identify and seize the one time coin that could best contribute to your overall time-coin wealth.

SELECT LIKE CORNETT
(STRATEGY VII)

So you are keen to start gaining or creating time-coin profits. How do you do it? Here is a helpful strategy:

1. Select and prioritize one of the costliest negative time coins.
2. Kickstart a timeful plan to eliminate or minimize its impact.

Remember—a timeful plan means creating a situation where the total time-coin profit for everyone involved is significantly higher than alternatives. A plan in which everyone comes up as winners, just like in the following case.

As Mayor Mick Cornett recounted in a 2013 TED talk, Oklahoma City had fallen far from its golden age.[43] By the early 2000s, it was absent from almost every ranking of America's top cities. It couldn't compete for "best place to live," "best for children," or any other desirable title. It drew little public interest and failed to attract new residents. Yet slightly before Cornett took office, the city had begun to recover. It started showing up on some of the lists, though always near the bottom. Except for one list where it reached the top: The fattest city in the U.S.A.

The mayor may have seen some obesity in town, but to be titled America's fattest city by Men's Fitness Magazine? Cornett uploaded his own height and weight to the website

---

43. Mick Cornett, *How an obese town lost a million pounds*, April 2013, TED Video, 15:02.

provided in the article.[44] He immediately got his BMI (body mass index) calculation and was in for a shock. He too was considered morbidly obese. Most mayors would have found the pressure of life too demanding to address the issue. They would have remembered an urgent call they had to take or run off to a meeting and forgotten about this obesity thing. At best, they might have turned down the doughnut they were offered at the next meeting.

But Cornett had a pretty good instinct for what would be a timeful investment. Something in his mind shifted. He realized he had struck gold, a significant cache of time coins. He decided to summon a film crew to the local zoo. With the world's largest land animal as a backdrop, he launched a huge campaign pledging that Oklahoma City is going to lose a million pounds.

Within less than a month, 51,000 residents signed up for the program Take it off Oklahoma! Noting that his city was also ill-suited for pedestrians, he promoted paving sidewalks and walking paths, creating new parks and improving existing ones, and even offered financial rewards to people who lost weight.

The campaign took off. Restaurants started offering special menus called "The Mayor Special," and talk in the media, the business community and people's homes began to revolve around physical activity and nutrition. In the end, residents lost much more than the planned million pounds, and Oklahoma City rose through the rankings as an athletic city.

What about the personal fortunes of the time wizard Cornett? He shed thirty-eight pounds and won much esteem and appreciation from his city, state and nation. Cornett can live knowing that he made a significant contribution, displayed

---

44. Men's Fitness magazine, 2007.

excellent timefulness, and put his city on a positive, upward trajectory.

As a result of this success, Cornett was also appointed President of the U.S. Mayoral Committee and won reelection as the Mayor of Oklahoma City, then he won it again and again and again.

ACHILLES' HEEL

Mick Cornett isn't the only one to influence a broad population by pushing a valuable idea to the top of the agenda. Many before him have done the same and set their community on a brighter path.

By focusing on weight lost and outdoor training, Cornett chose a highly valuable "time coin" that could benefit everyone. A coin that is expected to extend the life expectancy of the city's residents by up to 7.2 years while significantly contributing to their quality of life and minimizing their living expenses.[45]

Enthusiasm spread, as many residents were winning valuable time coins in the form of improved health and wellbeing, as well as taking part in a joint effort.

Perhaps the most remarkable lesson we can learn from Cornett's case is that we can do anything. At least anything we can think of. The result will not always be a completely identical copy of our vision, of course, but it will usually be close enough. If we think of ourselves only as a mayor, shoe seller, banker, CEO, scientist, or a president, this vision will probably

---

45. Steven C. Moore et al., PLOS Medicine plus common sense (regarding quality of life and expenses).

limit what we achieve. But how much more would we be able to achieve if we envision ourselves as people who are, in fact, engineering human time?

At the end of the day, all that most of us are born with are the days of our lives. We gradually learn to trade time for other things such as knowledge, skills, property, happiness or the joy of giving. But our most important achievement is our ability to gain ever-growing control of our own thoughts, adopt preferable thoughts, and bring these thoughts to the fore for other people, too. This ability to choose how we think about the world allows us to imagine more time coins than any other life form and convince ourselves and others of their value.

In this way, we can persuade the good people of Oklahoma City that—though boosting employment, improving education, and supporting culture may be important—losing weight is the most important time coin right now.

Similarly, we can persuade ourselves or others that one of the most important things in life is whether our smartphone is truly smart or that few things in life are more important than whether our phone bears an Apple logo or a Samsung one. Whether we wear a crucifix or star of David. Whether we believe in Muhamad or Jesus, one God or many.[46]

Some of these are, of course, quite important. Some probably are less so. But all of them are labels, and our tendency to think in labels can be an Achilles heel. Because these labels so easily distract us from seeing the deeper truth—that our life is our time. If we substitute even one less valuable label, narrative, belief or claim for a more valuable one, we have already taken our first step towards a more timeful life.

---

46. Inspired by Yuval Noah Harari, *Sapiens*, HarperAudio, New York, 2017.

###

If you followed some goal relentlessly, mainly because it's a trendy label and realized it's an empty shell offering very little value, share it with our community of time wizards. Use #timefulness #timewizard #achillesheel.

SELECTION EQUALS ADAPTATION

To become as successful as she can, Emily decides to create and spread timefulness wherever she is. But she also knows she must avoid timefulmess. Emily tries to think of a few time crimes. Her neighbor upstairs springs to mind. The one who moves his furniture around all day (and a fair portion of the night). She also thinks of the nice elderly woman on the first floor who declines to clean up after her dog by explaining (with an adorable smile) that back pains keep her from being able to bend down. She once even asked Emily to help do the honors. The request felt so odd and brave that Emily agreed. It was not a pleasant experience. "If I had stepped in that," thinks Emily, "that would have been a real timefulmess incident." Emily protects her time coins when she is in her apartment by using noise canceling headphones and keeping a good eye out for messes on the sidewalk. However, these cases are fairly obvious (like the clear positive and negative time coins). These are the time coins we are all quite good in avoiding from. But how about the challenging cases which are not always easy to flag as opportunities to think and act timefully?

Emily remembers her interview for her current job at Eitan Group (formerly Q Core Medical). At the end of the interview, Boaz, the CEO, asked if she had already been interviewed by

HR. When she answered in the negative, he asked a second question:

"Who interviewed you, then?"

"Yael and Shaul," answered Emily.

"Can you wait here a minute?" Boaz requested. "I'd like you to talk to Yulia, our head of HR."

He called Yulia's extension, but no one answered. He got up and muttered to himself, "I can't stand it when people aren't where they should be!" and walked off to look for Yulia.

Then something happened that Emily had rarely seen, especially not when dealing with senior leadership. Boaz stopped at the door, turned around, and apologized:

"Enough people have talked to you. If we can't make a decision, we don't deserve to live. Thank you for coming. We'll update you later this evening."[47]

Emily got the job. But she also gained something no less precious: A glimpse into the mind of a serially successful person. Someone she had learned to recognize as one of Israel's top corporate leaders. A tough combat pilot who survived three years in Syrian captivity, completed his Ph.D. in physics, worked for Intel, held one of the key patents for flash memo-

---

47. In English, you would expect the CEO (Boaz) to say something like "we have very little future here," or "the company could die." You might even attribute Boaz's language to the fact that he spoke in Hebrew, which is a more direct language (for good and for bad). Perhaps there is some timeful magic in a language that is characteristically thirty percent shorter compared with English. But language and culture aren't the only thing to note here. I have always found Boaz to share much commonalities with Musk. One good example for their common language and worldview is a reference coming from Walter Isaacson's biography of *Elon Musk* (Simon & Schuster Audio, Sep 12, 2023), in which Musk is quoted saying "I believed that if we couldn't do it in three [referring to SpaceX launches], we deserved to die." Boaz and Musk were both acting in what we are calling here "survival mode" (which Isaacson sometimes refer to as demon mode).

ry, sold a company for $400 million, has five highly successful, happy kids and eighteen grandchildren. Boaz and his wife, who is no smaller success than he is, recently purchased a bankrupt medical device company, which Emily just joined. It will be worth $1.4 billion in just a few years' time.

And in that glimpse into his behavior, unique and uncharacteristic for people of his rank, Emily had seen how he simply turned one perspective into another. Instead of sticking to preexisting processes (and his accessible thoughts), finding Yulia, and asking her to provide a fourth opinion, he deployed a new and far more efficient and success-oriented perspective about a start-up simply not having the "luxury" of overly long and costly processes. If he fails to apply the more timeful perspective, the startup could die. Interestingly, Emily felt that Boaz was talking not just about the start-up, but about his own mission in life and that of everyone else at the company.

Boaz, she then realized, had performed the exact magic that mayor Mick Cornett did, the magic she was after. Right in front of her eyes and with his own words, he not only changed his perspective but also shifted into survival mode. For a moment, Boaz no longer seemed to be running a hiring process. He appeared more like the captain of an airplane having to make a fateful decision here and now with no more than a minute or so to consult his crew.

Emily now asks herself what perspectives she can replace with a more timeful one. And how far could it take her if she looked at this shift like her life depended on it? Simply for the obvious reason that her life does depend on it...

"Well, there was this idea that I have to match my socks or can't have a housekeeper," she thinks, "but I got rid of both of those ideas. But there are still many other 'stories' that cost me time or diminish the quality of the time I do have. Stories I will soon rewrite."

YOUR EVOLUTION

Whatever you select, invent or work on, you'll eventually need to adapt it—you'll need to adjust your accessible thought and replace it with another, more timeful one. You can think of this change as your evolution. If evolution is the survival of the fittest by coincidental adaptation, human evolution—your evolution (and success), depends on the adaptation you'll choose to make during your life's critical crossroads—those "gold or coal" moments as we named them earlier. Differently than the evolution Darwin discovered, your evolution is in your hands. It's your choice. Make it a timeful one.

###

Use #timefulness #myevolution to share with our community of time wizards how you shifted from one modus operandi to a more timeful one—how you adapted and succeeded.

CHAPTER RECAP

- By pushing a valuable idea to the top of the agenda, you can set yourself and your community on a brighter path.
- Finding an idea that will lead to success isn't always easy, but there are four rules of thumb: (1) Don't think in labels—remember that at the end of the day it's time coins and time-coin wealth that we are after. (2) Once you do find an idea, ask yourself, how many more time coins will it return for your investment? (3) Once you find that valuable idea, you'll sometimes need to label it attractively, making it easy for you or others to sense how valuable it is. (4) Spread some time coins along the challenging way toward success making the journey easier for you or others.
- Our tendency to think in labels can be an Achilles heel, because labels can easily distract us from seeing the deeper truth—that our life is our time.
- Envision yourself as a person who is, in fact, engineering human time. Someone who can do everything—as long as it generates enough time-coin gains.
- Being able to shift from one modus operandi to another is a superpower that can boost our probability of success.
- Survival mode is when we muster all our might and act as if our life depends on it.
- Having the right perspective in life is worth a lot, but it's so much more powerful to hold the right perspective and move ahead on the right gear.
- If you want something done, act as if your life depends on it.

PART II RECAP

PART I	
Unlock Timefulness: Your Ultimate Key to Success.	
PART II	
Master Timefulness: Seven Strategies to Transform Your Life and Career.	
5.Focus Like Jobs	Focusing on one single time coin while sacrificing or deprioritizing others is a key to success. If you're not a one-time-coin person, that's OK. Just remember that there are times when we all have to focus on just one thing, at least for a little while.
6. Produce Like Picasso	Stop and think about a way of doing things differently. A way that will change the scale of your effectiveness, production scale and success.
7. Capitalize Like Franklin	It's all about time and the quality or meaning you find in it. Look past labels, projects and professions. If what you're working towards will result in greater time-coins wealth, go for it. If not, replace it or leverage it to gain something that will.
8. Lead Like Schwab	Be mindful. When opportunity calls, say "YES!" to the timefulness challenge. Greater risk and difficulty of a positive challenge can lead to a greater prize, as long as the risk is manageable.
9. Envision Like Musk	Create value by inventing new sources of time coins. If your inventions outstrip the alternatives, you've created an irresistible time coin that could tilt your time-coin flow or that of others—a phenomenon known as disruption. But you don't always have to overthink it. If you are creating positive time coins and avoiding the negative ones—you've done your share.
10. Futurecast Like Buffett	Invest in a predictable future or follow a serially successful person, company or a group that does. Focus on key time coins to enable other time coins to fall into place.
11. Select Like Cornett	Select a costly negative time coin and eliminate or minimize its impact. Aim for the biggest time coin gains—engineering human time (yours or others'). When needed, adapt and/or shift to survival mode.
PART III	
Beyond Strategies: Become Serially Successful.	

MAKE IT YOUR OWN

So, how do you go through the five steps we presented in Part I and choose the right strategies from those you read about in Part II? Here is an example relevant to many people. Just remember, it's only an example. It's up to you to choose the time coins and strategies most suited to your unique life circumstances—the only rule is that whatever you choose, it has to be timeful.

STEP 1: PREDICT

Let's say you've experienced some degree of disappointment, even frustration, over your daughter's use of social media. You feel that she could use her time more wisely. With these feelings and thoughts, your brain is signaling: "Hey, this is an opportunity to gain or lose time coins!" Give it some deliberate thought. Can you imagine how much better her life might become if she invests a few social-media hours in something more worthwhile?

STEP 2: SELECT OR INVENT

After you've categorized the opportunity (in this context, a challenging positive time coin), place it on the Time-Coin Tree (use figure 5). In doing so, you'll gain a better sense of how valuable the opportunity is compared to other options. Placing the coin on the tree will also help you visualize the scope of the needed investment and potential reward. The higher you place it on the tree, the tougher it will be. And the larger the time coin, the more positive (or negative) it is.

Figure 5: Your *Time-Coin Tree*

After categorizing or quantifying your opportunities, name them and place them on your *Time-Coin Tree*. By visualizing these opportunities, you'll gain a better sense of the relative value of each opportunity compared to other options you have or could create. This visualization will also increase your awareness to the various investments, gains, winning probabilities, potential losses, and risks associated with each opportunity (capturing the five parameters of our success formula). Remember, the higher you position an opportunity on the tree, the more challenging it might be, while the size of the time coin represents its potential positive or negative impact.

Alternatively, you can express the opportunity using the success formula. If you can't predict all the parameters, don't worry—good time wizards assume and presume as needed. Let's assume you're able to invest no more than fifteen minutes in completing this task. In so doing, you hope to save your daughter about two and a half hours out of the four she spends on social media every day, or at least make those hours more meaningful. Let's take a moment to emphasize a key point here. Even now, before you've started thinking about how you're going to tackle this challenge, by quantifying it, you've already gained a better sense of its potential impact. After all, if you realized that investing fifteen minutes could yield as much as ten times that for your child, you're both already potentially extremely successful. You're now ready for step three.

STEP **3**: INVEST

Make a table of the Seven Strategies. List the strategy in the left column of the table. Write down the ways you might implement the strategy on the right. The following is an example. You are welcome to use it for your personal and professional purposes and adjust it as needed.

STRATEGY	IMPLEMENTATION
Focus Like Jobs	To identify your daughter's potential "ace" time coin, consider the following: Is there something valuable that can capture her attention as much or even more than what she is currently doing? Devote about five minutes together to listing moments where you saw your daughter light up with excitement or immerse herself in a state of flow. If you both don't feel like you have some strong options, consider expanding your list by requesting ChatGPT or other similar AI tools to offer ideas which carry similarities to the things you know she likes. Then, select the one(s) that she can spend the most amount of time on and gain the highest total quality of time from. Devote ten minutes to thinking of ways to make those options more accessible to her: First finding great gymnastics or dancing classes, debate clubs, summer camps, audio books or podcasts she can listen to and helping her enroll. Repeat the process every now and then until she finds her "ace" time coin—until she finds herself.
Produce Like Picasso	Picasso and Einstein were creators more than consumers. Ask your daughter to consider if there are valuable things she can create (in or outside of social media). For instance, maybe she likes taking photos—maybe she can think of some unique theme common to all her photos, stories or posts. Then, try finding ways to boost the pace of these creations and alter them—learning from each creation and gathering feedback. If the pace of the creation and adaptation she makes is high enough (and enjoyable enough), it's only a matter of time till she nails it.
Capitalize Like Franklin	One remarkable thing that Benjamin Franklin did was to ask himself (proactively): "What good can I do today?"[48] With some small video production or a touching story, your daughter can change the life course of numerous people (though one could be as precious as many). Guide her to start her day by proactively selecting the valuable content that she'll consume or create—let it be her own choice, not the algorithm's. Maybe she only wishes to make it a timeful Sunday tradition rather than a daily challenge. In either case, help her become a time coin printer—just like Franklin was.

---

48. Walter Isaacson, *Benjamin Franklin*: An American Life (New York, Simon & Schuster Audio: 2011).

Lead Like Schwab	When Charles Schwab wrote "6" on the factory floor, he set a standard and clarified for everyone the task at hand. Similarly, social media also holds benchmarks (likes, views, screen time, etc.). But some of them might be the wrong metrics for her (and maybe for some of us too). Devote fifteen minutes to deciding with your daughter how she wants to measure her success or track her goals—the ones she holds dear. Then make a content-consuming or a content-producing plan that will help her reach her target—for instance, becoming a better photographer. Guide her in monitoring and growing her success based on the metrics she values, metrics that will boost her time-coin wealth and possibly others' too. Give her an early opportunity to become a leader like Schwab.
Envision Like Musk	No need to invest $90,000 like Musk did, or cut the Mac's boot time like Jobs. Your daughter can come up with her own vision too. Our success formula could come in handy here. She can seek inspiration from countless people. One of them is Suvir Mirchandani, a fourteen-year-old who measured and weighed letters of different fonts and concluded that the U.S. government could save almost 400 million dollars a year by changing the font of government documents.[49] Help her think big like Musk and Mirchandani would.

---

49. Madeleine Stix, "Teen to Government: Change Your Typeface, Save Millions," CNN, March 29, 2014, https://edition.cnn.com/2014/03/27/living/student-money-saving-typeface-garamond-schools/index.html.

Futurecast Like Buffett	Social media algorithms are extremely sophisticated and can offer highly valuable content. They can offer (and even create) personalized content especially made for us. The problem is that there is no fixed "us," We are an ever-evolving entity. When we are tired, we might want one thing. When we're energized, another. Consider creating an additional timeful profile with your daughter (and perhaps one for yourself too) to cultivate more than one self. Maybe creating a Buffett-like sage profile would serve her or you nicely. Think carefully about whom "Buffett" would follow if he were on social media. Guide your daughter as she tries out a Buffett-like mentality while consuming, cultivating and creating the time coins she wants. Or maybe she would like to call her profile "The Oracle of (wherever you live)" and practice making forecasts. In parallel, let her have another profile—let's call it "Fun Buffett"—that she can use every once in a while, to let loose or enjoy less intense content. After all, a few small challenging negative time coins like the Coke Buffett drinks every now and then can also contribute to her time-coin wealth. Suggest that she sets her first Buffett profile on her home screen, making it more accessible than her "Fun Buffett" profile. The idea of using Buffett is just an example to get her inspired with an identity that can help her develop timefulness. If it would work better for her to imagine herself as "Oprah Winfrey," "Melinda Gates," "MacKenzie Scott," "Gandhi," "Nelson Mandela," "Marie Curie" or "Muhammad Ali," that's great. She should do whatever is timeful for her.
Select Like Cornett	Mick Cornett's magic was that he stumbled upon one of the most negative challenging time coins in his city and effectively addressed it. Let your daughter consider a challenging negative time coin on the web or in the real world and find a creative way to address it, perhaps minimizing or even eliminating its impact. If Cornett was able to ignite a one-million-pound weight loss campaign in 2013, just think of the campaigns and impact your daughter—and in fact each and every one of us—could and maybe should ignite. Now ask yourself if you should commit to investing those fifteen minutes to make it all happen? If it's in your power to tilt the time-coin flow in your family, and perhaps more than that, will you allow yourself not to? And if you do start to think along these lines, perhaps you can also better understand people like Cornett, and Musk—the serially successful—perhaps in time you'll join them, if you haven't already…

STEP 4: COLLECT AND REFLECT

If your daughter ended up spending her time more fruitfully, celebrate together. Then reflect and try to find ways in which you can use the seven strategies above to promote other causes and opportunities you have—collecting and reflecting, reflecting and collecting.

STEP 5: REPEAT

Once you succeed in such opportunities and focus on their common factor—time and its value—you can find similarities to other opportunities, repeating and leveraging your past successes to create more and better ones.

BECOME

Perhaps more important than everything thus far, is that as you go through this process, you become more timeful. Just like Buffett wouldn't waste his time, you shouldn't either. Making wrong choices or stopping when challenged is no longer an easy option for you. Continuing to rack up successes is, though. You have shifted from a student to a master—a master time wizard.

CHALLENGE YOURSELF AND OTHERS

You and the people dear to you will demonstrate a keen scent for where life's valuable time coins are. In time, if you are truly aware and alert, you can capture those crucial "gold or coal" moments, setting yourself and others up for success and happiness, changing lives forever.

###

Once you have put in the couple of hours needed to assemble a table like the one we discussed, or perhaps just a few minutes to address some other topic, share your plan with others. This will increase your commitment and help them hit a valuable target too. Use #timefulness to inspire people with your plans and the strategies you choose to use.

PART III

BEYOND STRATEGIES: BECOME SERIALLY SUCCESSFUL

MASTER YOUR
INNER COMPASS
A GUIDE TO TIMEFUL
DECISION-MAKING

Emily remembers how she divided life events into positive and negative time coins after the picnic with her sister Sarah. In cases of clearly positive or negative time coins, she, like all of us, knows what to do.

But how can she recognize a complex time coin when she faces one?

She starts by formulating one simple question which she expects could guide her when considering an opportunity: "Am I facing a sock pile—a potential "gold or coal" moment worthy of greater thought?"

As Emily gives it a thought, dinnertime arrives. Emily and her roommate John make spaghetti bolognese. It's delicious. Once again, she gets carried away and overeats and feels uncomfortable, but promises herself that tomorrow will be different.

The next morning, however, is a friend's wedding day. Emily finds herself standing in front of a beautiful Italian buffet. Last night's determination to be stricter about her diet has been forgotten. On an empty stomach, she feels and thinks quite differently. Emily wants cake.

As she reaches the dessert table, a tall, handsome Italian man approaches too. He smiles and starts making small talk. She starts to feel it—a warm tingly feeling, her heart beats a little faster. The attention feels good. And suddenly a realization wakes her from this little dream.

"It's my heart!" she thinks. "One of my most powerful tools is my heart." Emily believes in simple solutions. "I can't just stop in the middle of everything and start calculating the costs, potential gains, and risks involved in investing in an opportunity," she reasons. "There's got to be a better way. One that works for me."

Emily thinks her heart is a bit like a compass. And normally, it's pretty accurate—its north is a true north—and she can rely on it to guide her towards the right decision.

Sometimes, however, Emily's compass seems to lose its bearings. It points north, but "north" is no longer true north. A tempting opportunity to win an immediate, effortless good time, for example, can send her off in the wrong direction. In such cases, Emily's compass (her heart) points her towards something that feels like a worthy goal but could be a trap. A negative time coin that's challenging because it masquerades as a positive one. Similarly, considering a long-term, significant investment disrupts her compass from pointing north too. In those cases, her heart causes her discomfort, fear or stress.

How can Emily protect herself from falling prey to immediate gratification? Can her mind intervene in the workings of her heart?

Back to the man at the wedding, when they finish their brief chat, he turns away and walks straight to a woman—his soon to be wife, as it turns out. Emily realizes what has just happened. Seeking to recover from her embarrassment, she takes a cup of coffee, finds a quiet corner, and pulls a notebook out of her purse. She crosses her legs and looks once more at the question she wrote down. She sketches the following flow chart hoping to formulate a system she can count on.

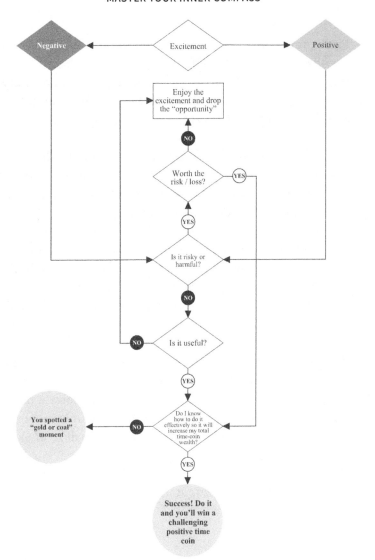

Figure 6: Opportunity Analysis
An emotion is a signal for an opportunity to gain or lose time coins. But the intensity or even the valence of the emotion could mislead us, preventing us from gaining more time-coin wealth and all in all a better life. This flow chart allows to rethink the directions we may want to take at life's critical crossroads—those "gold or coal" moments as we've named them.

Emily now believes she can do better. Equally important, she realizes that when she does get excited, it's because she faces a crossroads (a "gold or coal" moment)—an opportunity to increase or decrease her time-coin wealth. Being mindful of this and stopping to ask what the timeful choice would be can make all the difference, she now sees.

Emily feels she can move on to the next level now. She wonders how should she act in a situation where she's identified a challenging time coin that's likely to yield worthwhile fruits, but only after significant investments.

She recalls reading a quote by the 18th-century British portraitist and curator Joshua Reynolds: "There is no expedient to which a man will not resort to avoid the real labor of thinking."[50] "Not the most flattering saying," Emily thinks. But she takes comfort in the fact that even one of history's greatest and most prolific inventors, Thomas Edison, found Reynolds' quotation significant enough to display it prominently on his desk and throughout his laboratory. Thus, he reminded himself and his employees—including Nikola Tesla and Henry Ford—that when we flinch, tire, strain our thoughts, can't solve a problem, or feel thirsty, hungry, or tired, the opportunity may not lie where the compass needle points. Rather, a dose of extra thought could be in order.

Emily looks again at the bottom left of her sketch and adds the missing part of the puzzle stating "Extra thought":

---

50. "AERONAUTICS: Real Labor." *Time*. December 8, 1930. Archived from the original on January 25, 2008.

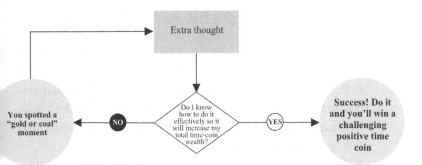

Figure 7: Extra thought
When facing challenging time coins, a dose of extra thought could enable you
to make the better choice.

<u>CHAPTER RECAP</u>

- Feeling excited can mean we're facing an opportunity to increase or decrease our time-coin wealth.
- Being aware of our emotions and physical state is an intuitive way to recognize challenging time coins and the crossroads leading to them, opportunities which could end up as our "gold or coal" moments.
- Being mindful of our feelings and stopping to ask ourselves what would yield more time-coin wealth is the first step towards success.
- The stronger our response is, the more critical the crossroad we are facing might be. Nevertheless, the strength of our feelings or even their positivity (or negativity) doesn't necessarily point out the direction we want to take.
- If you're excited and perceive a huge, immediate win, it might be a sign to consider some of the other parameters of the success formula.
- Our mind can intervene in the workings of our heart to increase our chances of success. The recipe is simple: When getting excited, stop and ask yourself this: Will it increase my overall time-coin wealth?
- A dose of extra thought could be the solution not just to avoiding challenging negative time coins, but also to effectively win the positive ones.

DESIGNING YOUR LIFE
A STEP-BY-STEP GUIDE

Emily feels she got it. She has started to feel more confident with systematically implementing timefulness in her life. She now wants to tackle the two most valuable time coins she has in mind—her career and her significant other. She decides to implement the Five-Step plan to help her achieve her goals.

She starts thinking about her career. Is she really happy with it? Will it provide her with all the time coins she is after?

This is Step One—Predict: Emily needs to predict whether she'll be better off keeping her current job or looking for another. Emily is afraid—changing jobs can be hard. Her apprehension is the first sign of a potentially positive challenging time coin. But it's not the only valuable thing she can figure out. If she can figure out why she feels uncomfortable, she might be able to focus her time and effort on where the real challenge is.

After giving the matter some extra thought, she understands that most of her concerns revolve around the job interview. That slight anxiety in itself is a good reason to go for it. Emily completed Step Two—Select: She realized she was able to instinctively categorize the opportunity as a challenging positive time coin—she opted in.

She is now in Step Three—Invest: She needs to find an effective way to manage her investment—getting through the job interviews (and her concerns). As she sits at the wedding table watching the guests, she notices a young boy helping his grandfather make his way to their table. It looks like the grandfather's sight is not great. "It looks like he could have cataracts. I wonder why some people choose not to have cataract surgery," she thought. "Would I have it done if I needed to? Isn't it like changing a job nowadays in that it's a relatively safe operation? And is there a connection between the choice I'll make now regarding a job transition and my ability to decide on having cataracts removed sixty years from now, or even the way I'll select my next job or prepare for an interview and the way I'll select a surgeon one day when I might need one? Will the choice I make only shape my career, or will it shape my decision-making process, my patterns of behavior, my identity and my life overall?"

Thinking of the man's cataracts, Emily recalls a story she once heard about Confucius.[51] He was about to lose his eyesight to cataracts. Conducting an ophthalmological operation in the days of Confucius was fraught with risk. It could have easily failed. But Confucius' operation was successful. Equally important was that his method ended up being successful too. Confucius summoned fifty of the best Chinese doctors and fifty of the best foreign doctors he could find. At the same time, he invited a thousand people who needed cataract surgery. Following his instructions, each of the hundred doctors treated ten different patients. Confucius closely monitored the recovery of the patients. Then, he chose the doctor with the highest success rate for his own surgery.

---

51. The late President of the State of Israel, Nobel Peace Laureate and former Prime Minister of Israel, Shimon Peres, used to talk about the way in which Confucius dealt with cataracts and attributed to him the first proactive use of Big Data in medicine, as he told Eyal Gora, founder and former CEO of Zebra Medical, an AI company in the field of radiology. Proof for the authenticity of Confucius story as told by Peres couldn't be found by the author, meaning that the story could be a myth.

Confucius focused on choosing the right doctor—and invested time in collecting and analyzing the data that would lead him to this particular doctor. He put remarkable effort into the task. On the other hand, if we needed to see a doctor, we would probably visit the first doctor that springs to mind—someone a friend just recommended, or some famous practitioner, or whomever our insurance company covers—just like mating socks, we simply do it. Why not?

Emily thinks she's starting to understand "why not." Thinking about Confucius and the challenge she finds intimidating—an upcoming job interview—she brings her notebook closer and writes:

> <u>The doctor Confucius chose</u> = me, Emily—I should bring myself to become the best candidate for the job.
>
> <u>Ten surgeries</u> = ten simulation interviews I can make before the real interview.
>
> <u>Ten patients</u> = ten interviewers.
>
> <u>Cataracts</u> = anything that I must overcome during each of the preliminary interviews.

Emily scheduled ten simulation interviews. "That was a challenging investment," she thought, after scheduling the interviews. But she calculates that each simulation will add a year of experience to the impression she makes in the real interview.

The investment in finding mock interviewers in return for a favor to a friend or payment to professionals ended up being significant, but she knew it would be worth it. And it was: Emily got the job she was after. Surprisingly, she was also about ten years younger than the other two product managers at the new company she started working for. Emily now has a way. The way of serially successful people. A way leaving very little room for luck. Serially successful people don't wait for the stars to align—they set them up.

What Emily hasn't yet realized (though she soon will) is that Confucius' method isn't limited to a job interview for product managers or surgeons. The same method would be just as handy for writing her resume, becoming a better manager or improving in any field of her choice. The right dose of extra thought combined with effective effort could help her achieve almost anything. In the few cases that it doesn't, she will learn a valuable lesson on which she can build some other success. After all, from a timefulness perspective, failures also compound her time-coin wealth.

Emily is in Step Four—Collect and Reflect: After some time at her new job, she reflected on her progress and the way ahead. She could now make a far more adequate prediction regarding her current job and her next one. She didn't even need to think how she would get it—she already had a system in place, the required experience and the confidence that it would work.

She got to Step Five—Repeat: Emily worked for six more companies after her first challenging transition. Although twenty years have passed since that first transition, she can't know how much time-coin wealth she would have gained or lost if she hadn't initiated the first transition. She does know one thing though—she got all the time-coin wealth she could ask for since then.

She became such a good interviewee that she invited some of her closest friends and family members to visit her to do simulations before their interviews—they all reached the same level of success as Emily did. It was the method she (and they) used that worked the magic—not her own talents or ambitions. Theirs was the approach of a serially successful person, not a guarantee but a pretty good shot.

Emily doesn't perform ten simulation interviews anymore or think about how to present her past job or career for more than twenty minutes. She can do it almost intuitively—and you too. You can go through the same process. Mind you, not only in finding (and winning) your dream job, but when pursuing any valuable opportunity you are after.

Use #timefulness #transition to share how you successfully transformed your good job into an even more timeful one, or how you made a timeful transition.

CHAPTER RECAP

- In many of life's situations, we simply know what we should do. The question is—should we do it differently? Should we invest some extra thought, look for wisdom in analogous situations, or do some preparatory investment to secure our success or boost its scale?
- A more effective investment also means less room for luck.

LOVE LIKE LINCOLN
ROMANCE AND THE
SHORTCUT TO SUCCESS

While the previous chapter focused on Emily's career using our five-step plan to become timeful masters as described in Part I of the book, this chapter concerns Emily's love life (and perhaps ours too). It draws from the seven strategies outlined in Part II of the book, facilitating Emily's desire to find a partner.

When Emily broke up with her boyfriend after four years, she knew she'd get over it. But somehow, that breakup felt different from her previous ones. Very different.

When Emily started her first long-term relationship, she was twenty-one, but now she is thirty-one, and her third relationship, the one she just ended, wasn't in any way better than her previous two, which lasted three years each. What should she do to minimize the chances she'd get into the same situation ten years down the road—when she is forty-one? Emily likes to plan everything. She hopes to have her first child before she hits thirty-seven. Unfortunately, love life isn't like pairing socks, choosing an ophthalmological surgeon or preparing for a job interview, and it's certainly not like choosing a picnic over a restaurant. Or is it?

Considering that life is all about time and the way she chooses using it, why wouldn't Emily be able to implement the seven strategies in any field of her liking—even romance, with the appropriate adjustments of course. Emily pulls her notebook closer, flips to its last page and lists down the seven strategies and the ways she might be able to use them to come up with a plan that would be more likely to lead her to the love life she is after. She writes:

1. **Focus like Jobs:** My focus should shift from entering into another relationship and managing it to becoming a better judge of people's character, with an eye toward finding a good match for my own.

2. **Produce like Picasso:** Up to now, I only meet people through introductions from close friends. It's a solid approach; I trust my friends' recommendations, and I am open to giving their ideas a try. When I do, it always starts with an extended "honeymoon" period. But do I fall in love with the person or with the relationship? And why not consider more options? Picasso had well over 100,000 creations. Not all of them are great, but I only need one great option and wouldn't have to consider 100,000 potential spouses to find my partner. I don't even have to put more time into the process. It's enough to have a more effective way of doing it. Just having different thoughts in mind when observing people or reflecting on people I like and dislike could strengthen my instincts. "What can I find out about a person in three or four years that I wouldn't be able to discover with deliberate effort in a year or less? Maybe even a few weeks, if not a single date or a quick phone call?" she thinks. Emily realizes she now has time for the task, because she has a different method—one that enables her to examine more opportunities in less time.

3. **Capitalize like Franklin:** "Franklin didn't become Franklin in a single day. He built one investment on top of another, and I too will learn a lot from everyone I meet, and even

observe or just message with—I can become a better judge of people's character with every person I meet.

4. **Lead Like Schwab:** The remarkable thing regarding Schwab, Andrei or Emily's fathers' stories, is that they or their managers defined the key focus point—the metric that should be addressed or the challenge to be solved. Emily thinks she can do this, too, and that her metrics should be the number of people she communicates with when she senses a smile on her face, an elevated heartbeat or the sudden urge to wonder whether that person could be the one.

5. **Envision Like Musk:** As Emily envisions her plan, she feels dissatisfied. She can't run around considering every person she meets as a potential spouse, or make too great an effort to socialize—she'd find it all too overwhelming, perhaps even a waste of time. She is now a timeful person, right? She needs another incentive to make every such interaction feel valuable regardless of its impact on her love life. Emily wants to create another source of time coins. She gives it a thought and decides to write a blog about her journey, so she can better reflect on her experience and help other young people in a situation like hers. She even expects that if the blog becomes a success, she might have some more options to choose from. And she was right—she did have more options to choose from, and it didn't take ten years to find a wonderful husband.

6. **Futurecast like Buffett:** Emily didn't embarrass herself by practicing going out on first dates. Instead, she read a few books about dating and personal-growth. She predicts that by significantly increasing the number of her interac-

tions, while incorporating the advice she's read, she would enhance the quality of these interactions.

7. **Select Like Cornett:** Emily realized her dating skills were as lacking as her former interviewing abilities. But she learned to be a great interviewee, so surely she could become a better dater too. Her most negative time coin was her inability to make a great first impression. A negative time coin she successfully addressed—professionally and now personally too.

THE END GAME—A SHORTCUT TO SUCCCESS

Emily is happy with her plan and change of perspective, but remembers that not long ago, when she was standing very close to the groom, she wasn't consciously controlling the situation. She wonders what could help her resist strong temptations and stick to her plan.

She tries to recall a case where she got carried away. Aside from the spaghetti bolognese incident, and some TV bingeing, she remembers a time she went into the supermarket quite hungry and bought all kinds of things she really didn't need and shouldn't have spent money (or time) on. But this doesn't happen when she prepares a list. "Isn't it crazy?" Emily thinks. "When I go to buy anything more than milk, coffee and bread, I make a shopping list. But when I am 'shopping' for my second half, which involves far more time-coin wealth than groceries, I do very little reflection or preparation."

It's a bit like the Confucius story in which he made a preparatory investment instead of swiftly hiring the first doctor who came to mind. Confucius isn't the only one who was able to control his impulses (and accessible thoughts)—a trait that is common among serially successful people.

Emily thinks of Abraham Lincoln's famous saying: If I would have six hours to chop a tree, I would invest the first four in sharpening the axe.

"That's quite counterintuitive," she thinks. "I don't know anyone who would do something like that, especially not nowadays. If we have a task at hand that we can't postpone, we normally just do it, trying not to waste time. But did Lincoln waste time or did he save time? Instead of starting to date again, maybe I'd be better off thinking about whom I might like to date?"

Emily takes her notebook and writes a pretty long list: "Happy, energetic, kind, caring…"

Then remembering that it's sometimes better to focus on one thing, she adds a small asterisk with a focus point:

"If my heart pounds hard, it doesn't necessarily mean I should go for it. It's just a sign to take out my list."

The secret to Confucius' and Lincoln's successes lies not only in their ability to stop and think differently, but also in a preceding effective investment (PEI). The PEI can take the form of knowledge, experience, a check-list, an instinct we cultivate or any past success we can further leverage into a future one.

But is there a shortcut to success? How could we increase our chances in life when such investments are simply not possible? Emily realized that her reflection on Confucius and Lincoln was exactly what she was after—a potential shortcut to success: A way to make a previously inaccessible thought accessible—a way to think differently. It encouraged her to put in some extra thinking, but it also gave her a system to follow—a potential shortcut to success.

When facing a challenging opportunity, she needed a source of inspiration to draw on—some story, advice or idea in order to derive to her own circumstances. By observing examples and finding similarities, she could make better predictions, selections, inventions or investments—either by replicating her own successes or by drawing inspiration from the triumphs of others.

Although Confucius' success wasn't her own, she realized she could replicate it to her liking. We aren't just a giant standing tall on the shoulders of our former selves planning our future. We are also, as Newton originally said, standing on the shoulders of other giants—from Confucius and Lincoln to Jobs and Musk (and many others too). With that, we open ourself to a world of endless opportunities. Opportunities that allow us to become masters in finding similarities that fit our own style, preferences and life goals. These are thoughts and even emotions that can compete with our accessible thoughts and offer an alternative, very often, a more timeful one.

Share how you made your preceding effective investment (PEI) using #timefulness #lovelikelincoln # planlikeconfucius.

<u>CHAPTER RECAP</u>

- Some opportunities in life require a preceding investment. The impulse to surge ahead can lead us astray.
- Everyone is more successful at some things than with others. Many times, we can apply the same principles from one area of success (such as grocery shopping) to another (such as love life)—recognizing and adapting these similarities can act as a timeful shortcut to success.
- If it feels like you don't have enough time, it could be that you only lack a timeful way.

THE END GAME
YOUR TIMEFUL PATH
TO SERIAL SUCCESS

Up until now, you've probably lived your life well—perhaps very well. The main purpose of this book is to become a tool that helps you live it even better. In fact, the book's key goal is to enable you to do just that by following five steps:

1. **Predict:** Once you've recognized an opportunity or a shift in your feelings, stop and reflect. Consider categorizing the opportunity you are facing as one of the four time coin types. When in doubt, quantify it using the success formula. Remember that half the battle is stopping and identifying opportunities correctly. Properly predicting your gains (and other parameters of the success formula) will provide you the clarity you'll need to decide and act wisely.

2. **Select or Invent:** Once you have a strong sense of the road ahead, you can make a more informed decision or invent a preferable alternative. You can then dive into your opportunity with greater confidence.

3. **Invest:** Use some of the strategies introduced in Part II to improve your chances of success and scale your success to your liking.

4. **Collect and Reflect:** Enjoy the fruits of your success and reflect to strengthen your instinctive ability to recognize time coins and the profits they carry. This process will enable you to apply yourself in seemingly different fields by finding correlations to what you've already achieved.

5. **Repeat:** Use your past experience and successes to get to other similar successes or perhaps bigger and better ones. Leverage the fact that each repetition will further refine your prediction strength, decision making ability, and investing effectiveness. It will also enhance your capacity for invention and reflection, continuously enhancing your instincts and overall success potential.

By consistently following these five steps, you'll refine your ability to identify or create valuable time coins and determine the best ways to harness them—you'll become serially successful.

Sometimes, you'll need to quantify an opportunity. Other times, just categorizing it is enough. Eventually, you'll simply feel it. However, the important thing is that the more you categorize and quantify, the better you'll be able to feel it. And the more you categorize, quantify and feel, the more successful you'll become. It's as simple as that.

Remember, every step you take in life, every second that passes, is not only an opportunity to increase your time-coin wealth. It's also an opportunity to become more successful, continuously leverage yourself and the time-coin wealth you've amassed to make your life and the lives of your dear ones ever better. This is the elixir of life: continuously harnessing and creating more and better time. And the more you consider timefulness, the more natural it becomes, and the more successful you'll be.

<u>CHAPTER RECAP</u>

- If you are able to ask yourself only one question and in only a few of life's crossroads, ask yourself this: Is it timeful?
- Choosing and acting timefully will compound to preceding investment which you'll be able to leverage further.
- Embracing timefulness as a life perspective, habit, or motto will sharpen your intuition allowing you to reduce effort and uncertainties while seizing more valuable opportunities. It's a process bridging the gap between our not always available intellect to our readily available intuition—thereby enhancing our chances of success.

PART III RECAP

PART I	
UNLOCK TIMEFULNESS: Your Ultimate Key to Success.	
PART II	
MASTER TIMEFULNESS: Seven Strategies to Transform Your Life and Career.	
PART III	
BEYOND STRATEGIES: Become Serially Successful.	
12. Master Your Inner Compass	Feeling excited? You might be facing a critical crossroads—a challenging time coin that can be a "gold or coal" moment. But your excitement alone won't necessarily lead you in the right direction. Focusing on the value of the opportunity, its risks and how you are going to effectively gain its time coins could serve you better. To best deal with challenging time coins, an extra dose of thought is usually in order.
13. Designing Your Life	Not sure how best to deal with a challenging positive opportunity? Find an effective way by using one or more of the seven strategies presented in Part II, conduct a preceding investment, or just give it some extra thought looking for inspiration and similarities you can draw from. There is (almost) always a way.
14. Love Like Lincoln	Look for the timeful shortcut to success. Sometimes, it'll be a preceding investment (like sharpening your axe), other times an inspiring case, story or figure—finding and adjusting those similarities to fit your unique life circumstances and goals could act as a highly effective shortcut to greater time-coin wealth. Remember, if it ever feels like you don't have enough time, it could be that you are overlooking a timeful solution.
15. The End Game	Life is not about one time coin or another—it's about systematically gaining more positive time-coin wealth. Follow the five steps: Predict, select (or invent), invest, collect (and reflect) and repeat—not only until you succeed, but until you become a success.

MAKE IT YOUR OWN

Timefulness is a perspective that sees life as time and the quality or meaning you imbue that time with. If you choose to adopt such a perspective, with time you'll find that you have increased your affinity to the challenging positive time coins and decreased your attraction to the negative ones.

As time goes by, you'll reduce your reliance on "slow thinking" and success formulas and incorporate them within your intuition.[52] Doing so will boost your chances of success by taking you a step closer to effortlessly seizing opportunities before your time, mental energy or other resources drain or a window of opportunity shuts.

This process will reward you with one of the greatest powers the world can offer. It's the power Einstein himself described as the definition of a genius—having "a keen scent and the stubbornness of a mule." It's not that you'll stop using your analytical thinking, but you'll be more likely to follow your "ace" time coin even when you're less aware of it. You'll also be more likely to rise to the level of your intellect in the cases where many of us fall to the level of our instincts.[53] In essence, you'll be closing the gap between the two.

The best part is that as it becomes less analytical and more intuition-based, it becomes less of a science and more of an art. It becomes less of a concept you read about or a system you follow, and more of a tool you integrate into your own unique circumstances. It becomes yours.

---

52. Refers to Keith Stanovich, Richard West and Daniel Kahneman's description of system 1 and system 2 as discusses in Daniel Kahneman, *Thinking, Fast and Slow.*

53. Inspired by Archilochus and James Clear, *Atomic Habits,* Cornerstone Press, London, Penguin Random House UK, 2018.

CHALLENGE YOURSELF AND OTHERS

1. Fill in figure 8: Your Time-Coin Wealth. Focus on the positive time coins. Select one or more which you find valuable, invest, collect (and reflect) and then repeat—until you become as timeful as you wish to be.
2. Spend time studying the negative time coins to understand the risks to your time and life. Recalibrate yourself towards the real risks threatening your time-coin wealth.
3. Utilize AI's ability to "easily" find useful correlations. Consider sharing with ChatGPT or similar tools the things you enjoy, think highly of and find value and meaning in—along with those you dislike. Put special emphasis on explaining how you view your time and would prefer to use it in the short and long term. Then ask for suggestions for how to invest your time, build your relationships, career and more. Share your original plans and discuss options to improve them, or consider alternatives and upgrade your plan.
4. Pose the same questions you shared with your favorite AI tools to people you trust. Especially interesting will be to share your thoughts with people whom you consider to be serially successful.

Remember: Time-coin gains and losses accumulate. Every individual time coin "radiates" and influences some or even all of the other time coins we have or will have. Take a holistic approach: Focus on a specific time coin when needed, without losing track of the big picture and the impact that such a time coin can have on your entire life (make figure 8 your own roadmap).

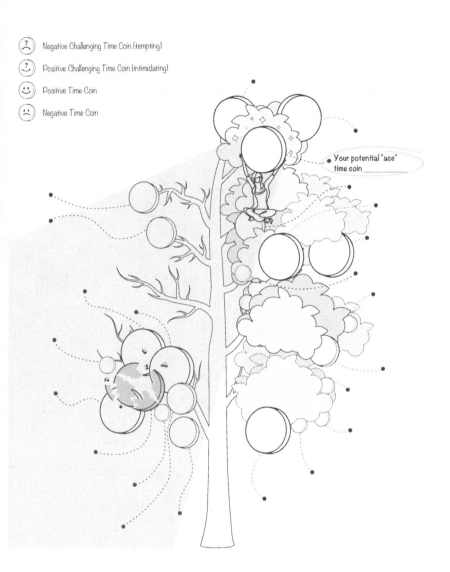

Figure 8: Your Time-Coin Wealth
Name your time coins to create the *Einstein Effect*—increasing the clarity of
the opportunities you pursue and the chances you'll get them.

###

Share your Time-Coin Tree with the people you love and care about, or with the world, letting others know where you believe the real treasure of life is. Use #timefulness #acetime-coin #realtreasure.

AFTERWORD

The serially successful people you read about broke through the barriers restricting their accessible thoughts. They offer countless valuable ways to provide us with greater time-coins wealth. But can we not look at our lives right here and now and do the same? Perhaps, like the paragons of success, we too can focus on the truly valuable time coins, those that increase our total time-coin wealth. Perhaps, all we need is a perspective enabling one simple, readily accessible question. That way, when it comes time to decide, to dedicate ourselves to our family, or work, to trade or invest, to love or to hate, we can stop for a short, precious moment and ask: What is the true worth of it? by how much would it increase our total time-coin wealth—our life? Put simply: Is it timeful?

Thank you for reading Timefulness. I hope you have found it insightful and helpful in your personal and professional life and growth.

If you have any questions or feedback, or want to learn more about how to implement timefulness in your life or businesses, feel free to reach out to Emily or Amir. You can contact them via their website at www.timeeconomy.com or email them at becometimeful@gmail.com. They would love to hear from you and continue the conversation on the importance of timefulness in our lives. Best of luck on your timeful journey towards a more timeful life!

Emily & Amir

CHALLENGE YOURSELF
AND OTHERS

Chapter 4
Share with the world your "gold or coal" moments and the cases where past investment allowed you to stand taller and reach higher. Use #timefulness #goldorcoal #bethatgiant #becomeasuccess.

PART I RECAP
Use #timefulness to share your discoveries, letting people know about quantified clear wins and alerting them to losses using #timecrime or #timefulmess.

Chapter 7
If you find something to be as valuable as one of Franklin's creations, something that others can "print" or join forces with you in an effective collaboration, please share it using #timefulness #timeprinting, or #printlikefranklin.

Chapter 8
When we repeat timeful choices, the greatest magic of all happens—we become ever more timeful and inspire others to become timeful too. Use #timefulness #toleadistobecome to share your stories of how you took a timeful decision, became timeful or lead an important initiative in a timeful manner.

Use #timefulleader to share examples of timeful leaders you admire—take a part in setting the standard we deserve.

Chapter 9
If you have such a vision in mind, use #timefulness #timeful-vision #envisionlikemusk to share your idea with our evolving timeful community.

Chapter 11
Use #timefulness #myevolution to share with our community of time wizards how you shifted from one modus operandi to a more timeful one—how you adapted and succeeded.

PART II RECAP
Once you have put in the couple of hours needed to assemble a table like the one we discussed, or perhaps just a few minutes to address some other topic, share your plan with others. This will increase your commitment and help them hit a valuable target too. Use #timefulness to inspire people with your plans and the strategies you choose to use.

Chapter 13
Use #timefulness #transition to share how you successfully transformed your good job into an even more timeful one, or how you made a timeful transition.

Chapter 14
Share how you made your preceding effective investment (PEI) using #timefulness #lovelikelincoln # planlikeconfucius.

PART III RECAP
Share your Time-Coin Tree with the people you love and care about, or with the world, letting others know where you believe the real treasure of life is. Use #timefulness #acetime-coin #realtreasure.

GLOSSARY

Accessible Thoughts: The immediate ideas, beliefs, or solutions that arise in one's mind, influenced by prevalent perspectives, current knowledge, shared societal concepts and an inclination to conserve energy and effort. These thoughts, often subconscious, shape behavior and decision-making but may not always represent the most optimal or comprehensive viewpoint.

Ace Time Coin: A particularly pivotal segment of time that, when given due attention and effort, can lead to exceptional positive outcomes and impact on our life or others'.

Challenging Time Coin: Periods of time requiring deeper contemplation due to their uncertain implications. These can be further divided into:

- **Positive Challenging Time Coins:** Time segments that, while demanding or uncertain, hold promise for positive long-term returns.
- **Negative Challenging Time Coins:** Moments that offer short-lived satisfaction but are likely to have detrimental long-term consequences.

Complex Time Coin: A multifaceted time period that holds both potential benefits and costs, demanding intricate analysis to determine its true value to us.

Confucius' Method: A strategy derived from the historical account of Confucius, where data and observation are used to make informed decisions. In the context of the book, it involves gathering data or practicing to become the best version of oneself for a particular challenge or opportunity.

Einstein Effect: The observation that when rewards and penalties are clear, especially in terms of time gain or loss, all humans tend to make the same efficient decisions.

Five-Step Plan: A structured approach or framework designed to help individuals, companies, states, or other human groups to predict, select (or invent), invest, reflect (and collect), and repeat their successes, or expand them to seemingly different fields in order to increase our total time-coin wealth.

1. **Predict (Step One):** The phase where we anticipate the potential outcomes of a decision, such as the implications of continuing with a current job versus seeking a new one.
2. **Select (Step Two):** The stage where we categorize an opportunity, often determining its nature, whether it's challenging, positive, or negative.
3. **Invest (Step Three):** The action phase, where we put in effort and resources towards achieving a goal, such as preparing for job interviews.
4. **Collect and Reflect (Step Four):** The introspection phase, where we evaluate the outcomes of our decisions and considers future steps.
5. **Repeat (Step Five):** The process of applying the gained knowledge and experience from previous steps to new opportunities or challenges.

"Gold or Coal" Moment: Decisive junctures where decisions can lead to substantial gains or losses in one's time-coin wealth.

Governing Principle (the Success Formula): A foundational built-in mechanism steering actions and decisions (as well as the general behavior, biology, chemistry and physics of humans and all other organisms) particularly aimed at protecting their time (life), the time of their offspring's, specie, contributing species and maximizing its value. This mechanism is evolutionary wired for effectiveness, but suffers from biases between survival and thriving (time and time quality), as well as other biases between the immediate, long term, overall time and our time compared to others'. And of course, a bias between an optimal result to managing time, risk, energy and other resources.

Magic of Time: The unique ability to invest a certain amount of time, thought, effort, or resources (collectively termed as "time coins") in a way that generates more value by saving or enhancing time for oneself or others.

Negative Time Coins: Instances of time that detract from our life's quality or overall life duration.

Positive Time Coins: Segments of time that resulted in a clear positive impact on our life, enhancing our overall well-being.

Preceding Effective Investment (PEI): An initial commitment, in the form of knowledge or resources, ensuring future success through foresight, planning, instinct, or intuition.

Serially Successful: The consistent and repeated achievement of success across various endeavors.

Serially Successful Factor: The degree of confidence that an action or investment will yield success.

Seven Strategies: A few key strategies used by the serially successful and described in the book Timefulness including:

1. **Focus like Jobs:** Prioritize one time coin, understanding that at times, success requires singular focus, even if temporarily.
2. **Produce like Picasso:** Reimagine your approach to boost effectiveness and scale, striving for transformative success.
3. **Capitalize like Franklin:** Pursue activities that amplify time-coin wealth, while demonstrating a continuous ability to change our field of focus, or leverage past success to create other successes—always focusing on our action's value.
4. **Lead like Schwab:** Embrace challenges mindfully. Greater rewards often accompany greater risks, provided they are calculated. Identifying, or framing an opportunity as the

key priority allows you to show the way to others or lead the effort of getting such well-defined time coin source.

5. **Envision like Musk:** Invent new valuable time coins. Outshine alternatives to disrupt the norm, ensuring a net positive time-coin outcome.

6. **Futurecast Like Buffett:** Align with a predictable future or those proven to do so. Prioritize key time coins to set others in motion.

7. **Select like Cornett:** Identify and reduce the impact of negative time coins. Maximize gains by optimizing human time, pivoting as needed to survive and thrive.

Time Coin(s): Metaphorical units symbolizing the product of time and its significance to us. Each coin represents a segment of time multiplied by its objective, or subjective value, or meaning, underscoring the potential impact of our choices.

Time-Coin Tree: A visual tool categorizing opportunities based on their relative time-coin value and cost incapsulating the potential impact of the five parameters assembling the success formula.

Time-Coin Wealth: The cumulative value of all the time we've experienced or utilized, both positively and negatively while influencing our potential for future growth.

Time Crimes (timefulmess**):** Actions that waste or misuse time, reducing one's overall time-coin wealth or that of others.

Timeful: Demonstrating a conscious or unconscious approach valuing time and its quality as the ultimate currency and tending to result in an overall increased time-coin wealth.

Timefulness (Time Economy): A mindful and strategic awareness (as well as an unaware tendency), favoring the intrinsic value of time, guiding one's actions and decisions to make the most out of their current and future time and life overall.

ACKNOWLEDGEMENTS

I have made a great deal of effort finding and quoting sources for this book. If I have made any mistake, or missed a source requiring a quote, or if any reader has information or comments regarding the text in this book, kindly contact Amir Peled at **becometimeful@gmail.com**. Your assistance in ensuring accuracy is greatly appreciated and I'll do my best to amend any potential mistake I might have done.

A special thanks to the readers of the first manuscripts who filled my heart with their hearts and illuminated my eyes with theirs:

My deep appreciation to the book's chief editor Tony Maxwell, who read the first English print, recognized its potential, and demonstrated an unmatched ability to streamline its language and provide deep insights where they were very much needed. Thank you Tony, for your guidance, goodwill, patience, wisdom, talent and style.

Special thanks to Dr. Efraim (Efi) Vitzrabin, who read every single one of the early drafts and contributed greatly to the book's success. Special thanks also go to Christian Leth Nielsen, who read the first English print and the prefinal first edition and guided me on how to make the book more valuable, accessible and impactful and did so in his very timeful way. To Dr. Yaron Frid, who added much needed empathy, talent and magic touch, and helped choose the very best intro to the book. And a special thank you to Magda Gendźwiłł, who provided deep insights and valuable criticism, which ended up adding the book its brightest star. Similarly, I would like to thank Anna Leah Berstein Simpson who helped throughout a long period and multiple versions. Thank you Anna, for your always meticulous proofreading, shrewd judgment and much valuable nuance regarding the American culture, proper use of the language and the addition of empathy and style which no book can get enough of.

Thanks to Tomer Peled, Tamar Naishlos, Omer Kirshenboim, Gil Rabbie, Dr. Jonathan Boxman, Orahn Preiss-Bloom, Elisabeth Mayman, Masha Nikolvski, Charna Ashkenazy, Dr Yaniv Mayer, Pinhas Mazor, Oded Rozenberg, Ziv Kirshenboim, Avihay Eyal, Asher Kirshenboim, Chen Gillon, Neri Minsky, Yaniv Aharon, Ronen Rabinovici, Jack Yulzari, Nir Levin, Yaron Tomer, Prof. Chaim Gutfinger, Tom Benjamin, Nissim Nehar Dea, Gili Karniel, Dr. Ronit Merchav-Feuermann, Dr. Taly Lindner, Prof. Haim Lotem, Moti Naishlos, Sharon Peled, and my dear friends Alessio Andreoli and Dr. Andrei Yosef who believed in me and the book.

My deep gratitude also to all those who read the manuscript professionally for their critiques and comments: Sivan Gal, Idit Nevo, Abigail Kantorovich, Tzippy Gurion, Rotem Biron, Ben Vered, Orna Landau, Shmuel Rosner, Dafna Harel Kfir, and Ronit Rosenthal and to Benny and Nave Carmi, Amir Philos and the eBookPro team, who lead me to make the book cover and messages far more timeful.

This book is dedicated to my parents Nurit and Yakov Peled, who gave me the gift of life; to my siblings Tomer and Yifat (Agate), who gifted me with vision and inspiration; to my children Tamar, Noam, and Shaked, for whom I wrote this book in the hope of making their world as good as it can possibly be.

A special thanks to Orit, my second half, for her endless support, encouragement and love.

And above all to God above.

Amir Peled

Made in the USA
Las Vegas, NV
14 December 2023

82748468R00085